E.A. Dustin

Save me Twice

Historical Fiction - Based on a true WWII story

Save me Twice
Copyright @ 2016
E.A. Dustin

Cover photo: Anabel Schk

Published by Verify, LLC

ISBN-13:
978-1537475073 (Save Me Twice)

ISBN-10:
153747507X

Library of Congress Cataloging-in-Publication Data
E.A. Dustin
    Save me Twice / by EA Dustin
    ISBN-13:
    978-1537475073 (Save Me Twice)

    ISBN-10:
    153747507X

1. World War II- Fiction 2. Concentration Camp Mauthausen 3.
    Holocaust – Fiction

Acknowledgments

There are many people to thank for the creation of this book and for helping me tell Karl's story. Thank you all for your patience and time.

Here is a list of those who provided valuable edits, feedback and insights:

Tracey Wong Briggs is a writer/editor; Linda Schaffer is an avid reader and book critic; Eve Pines is a businesswoman and a critical thinker; Janice Voth is a publications lead and editor; Erika Rashka is a hard working physicist and engineer with many artistic talents; Mary Russo is a medical technician with a keen eye for details; Jean James is retired with loads of wisdom; and Dan Gerber is my co-worker and a hobby historian. Thanks to Lynn Smith for choosing "Save Me Twice" as the book pick for book club and to all the other ladies who personally told me they chose this book for their respective book clubs.

I also appreciate the early feedback and encouragement from Lisa Pettrey-Gill, who is multi-talented; Rose Marie Sanders, who is an avid reader of WWII history; Jackie Dustin, who is hardworking, multi-talented, with amazing baking skills; my wonderful supportive siblings; and thanks to Cedric Dustin for the creative input.

Thanks to my editor Naomi Harward for the quality improvements.

Thanks to my Dad Karl who told me his story in verbal and written forms and who patiently answered many of my questions. Thanks for my Mom for all her patience.

I am truly grateful to each one of you and your inputs. You all live (and have lived) your lives with excellence.

Preface

University of Virginia professor Jerome McGann, during his October 4, 2016 "Thomas Jefferson" award and subsequent timely acceptance speech at UVA, Charlottesville, reminded members of his audience, including me, about Milman Parry's speech. Parry delivered the famous lecture "The Historical Method in Literary Criticism[i]" in 1934, the year before he died, to the Harvard Board of Overseers.

The important context of Parry's lecture is signaled by its date, 1934, when "propaganda...social changes and confusion" were taking such hold of bewildered people throughout Europe and America. Stalin had assumed control of the Soviets in 1923, Hitler of the Weimar Republic in 1933, and a freewheeling American Capitalism had plunged the United States into a tormented social condition. Parry reflected on that situation during his famous lecture of 1934:

The chief emotional ideas to which men seem to be turning at present. . .are those of nationality—for which they exploit race—and class. . .Anyone who has followed the history of the use of propaganda for political purposes, with its extraordinary development of intensity and technique in the past fifty years [recognizes how] those who were directing that propaganda expressed their lack of concern, or even contempt, for what actually was so, or actually had been so.[ii]

When Milman Parry gave his lecture then, he couldn't have imagined the magnitude of truth to his words and the horrific impact this propaganda that he had warned the Harvard Board of Overseers about would have in the next decade. Propaganda that exploited race and class helped Hitler become the Fuehrer. Millions fell victim to it. Karl's experience, described in this book, gives a glimpse of the historical consequences. Mainly, we owe it to humankind. And it is our responsibility to not let history repeat itself.[iii]

Chapter 1
Arrival

October 1944, Suburb of Nürnberg

"What was that?" Karl jolted up his head from his pillow, holding his breath as he searched for the source of the noise. His heart was beating out of his chest. Then he heard it again clearly—another impatient banging at the front door, this one even louder than before.

He heard his mother in her slippers hurrying down the squeaky, wooden steps winding toward the front door.

"Who is it?" she asked in a shaky voice. Karl could hear the fear in it. He jumped out from under his warm down comforter, swept aside a strand of red curls off his forehead, and hurriedly tip-toed to his bedroom door to press his ear against it.

"SS! Open the door!" ordered a harsh, deep voice, accompanied by even more impatient banging.

"SS!"

Karl knew the SS was the German *Schutzstaffel*, soldiers known for their organized oppression under Hitler's iron fist. What he didn't know at the time was the extent of the brutality through which the SS ruled. They ruthlessly blundered and murdered indiscriminately in the name of protecting Hitler. Anyone who disagreed with the Nazi propaganda or stood in their way would be eliminated. Some were lucky enough to just get shot; many others were tortured, or decapitated.

Immediately Karl thought of his good friend Daniel, the son of the Morgenthau's—a Jewish family in their village who had recently tragically disappeared. Everyone had suspected the SS.

Who were the SS here for? What were they doing at his family's doorstep this late at night? What could they possibly want? Karl's family stayed pretty much to themselves; they had been model citizens. They had no choice, really—these days, nobody dared to be anything else. And ever since Albert, their Hitler Youth leader, and former childhood friend, had insisted they attend all Hitler Youth meetings, Karl and his brother Hans had not missed one.

A scary thought crossed Karl's mind: *Was it Mom's radio?* They must have caught on to it. He had told her many times to turn that darned thing off. He should have thrown it away. Why else would the SS be here this late at night? Citizens were forbidden to listen to anything else but the *Reichssender* (national radio station), but lately, she had tuned in to other, non-German stations, called the "*Feindsender*" (enemy station). She had made sure to keep the volume down so low that nobody from outside could hear it, but Karl knew that they still could have traced it. What else could it possibly be?

Whatever it was, something was very wrong. Karl's mind continued to race. *Were they bringing news about his missing uncle? Of course not... Not this late, in the middle of the night.*

He heard the squeaky opening of the heavy oak front door. The small old bell that hung over it chimed with a dull sound.

"Heil, Hitler!" He could hear the clicking of heels of at least two soldiers. He could imagine them standing there: both in their 30's, armed, tall and grim, with their arms extended for the Hitler salute.

As one of the soldiers began to speak, Karl immediately recognized his voice: *Albert!* The familiar voice of their childhood friend echoed down their quaint entranceway.

"Frau Elheusch, where are Hans and Karl?" Albert demanded.

Karl gasped. They were here for him and his older brother. To take them to war. *Impossible! Why? What difference could they make at this point?* So many lives had already been lost. Germany was on the retreat from all sides, especially the Eastern front. The German *Wehrmacht* was rapidly running out of recruits. Karl had heard the call for all boys from age twelve and up to join the war. And now the SS were here to collect them.

Karl rushed over to Hans's bed only a few feet away. He could barely see, save for the dim light seeping through the crack of his bedroom door that aided him in the dark. *Mutter* had turned on the air raid light bulbs, which was all that was allowed during the "darkening law", in case of an air raid.

As Karl reached his brother's bed, he shook Hans by the shoulder. "The SS is here! They are here for us!" he whispered frantically, trying to wake his brother. But after an exhausting day of herding cows, Hans was in a deep sleep.

"Hmhm," was the only response as Hans rolled back over.

Karl ripped off the warm, white bed cover. "Wake up!" He muffled a frustrated growl, desperate to wake his older brother without making too much noise.

At the same time, Karl could hear his mother's pleading, high-pitched voice: "The boys are asleep. What do you want from them? Please, Albert, not my boys. They are only children. Not tonight. Come back tomorrow." She started to ramble. Karl couldn't make out all the words, but her cries were getting louder.

"They are children, please don't take them!" she continued to beg. Then Karl heard shuffling noises—she was trying to prevent them from going upstairs. Suddenly she cried out, and then the hurried footsteps drew closer until the soldiers' heavy boots stopped in front of the boys' bedroom. The door to their room flew open, and the same commanding voice Karl had heard downstairs bellowed: "Heil Hitler! Get up!"

Karl heard the heels clicking, and then a flashlight powered by a hand generator shot its beam at them. These flashlights remained lit as long as the soldier squeezed the spring-loaded hand-piece. Squinting and shielding his eyes with his hand as they adjusted to the bright stream of light now glaring into their dark bedroom, Karl managed to make out the dark silhouettes of two soldiers standing in the door—one much taller than the other—with their weapons over their shoulders, powerful and brazen, their arms extended as part of the "Heil, Hitler" sign.

"Heil Hitler!" Karl answered, jumping to extend the Hitler salute, and clicking his bare heels together on the cold bedroom floor. Then, in an attempt to calm the situation, he dared to ask, mustering up the most charm possible given the eerie situation: "Hallo, Albert. How are you?"

"I am SS-Scharfuehrer Wuest to you!" Albert barked. The shadows falling on his face made the frown lines on his forehead appear much deeper than the last time Karl had seen him.

"Get dressed!" demanded the shorter SS soldier, pacing swiftly. Karl didn't recognize this sandy-brown haired soldier.

"We have orders," he was saying. "You are to come with us! You are joining the SS. You will serve your *Vaterland*! Heil Hitler!"

"Why tonight? Can't you come back in the morning?" Mutter cried in vain from behind the men.

"Wake him up!" Albert demanded, his head gesturing toward Hans. "Mmmm." More unintelligible mumblings came from the sleeping Hans.

"Hans, wake up!" Karl grabbed his brother's shoulder again.

"What?" The older boy slowly sat up, looking around at the scene, dazed, trying to make sense of the ruckus.

As he fully awoke, he noticed the red SS patch on the soldiers' arms, reflecting in the light. He scooted his body back toward the headboard, away from the glaring light. Why were these SS soldiers in his house? Then he heard Karl ask the soldiers what they should pack.

"Where are we going?" Hans asked incredulously.

Instead of responding, Albert went on to demand, "Where is Hermann?"

Their other brother. Shocked, Karl responded, "Why do you need Hermann? He can't do anything for you or to serve the Vaterland. You know he is in a wheelchair. Why don't you leave him be?"

Albert glared down at Karl. "We have orders to take him, too. We have to take him to a home," he said coldly.

"A home? He doesn't need to be in a home. He is fine here!" Karl responded, feeling more fear now for the well-being of his handicapped brother than for himself.

Without a word, Albert headed toward the next bedroom. He knew this house inside out—he had spent much time here just a few years back. He found Hermann in his bed wide awake, roused from his slumber by the ruckus in the other room. Hermann had always been a light sleeper. He squinted, adjusting to the flashlight now being pointed at him.

"Hermann, get dressed," Albert demanded. "You are coming with us."

Then he turned to the other SS. "Gefreiter Ferdinand, once Hermann is dressed, carry him downstairs and put him in his wheelchair!"

Ferdinand hesitated, seeming puzzled. With a lowered voice, he leaned in toward Albert. "Albert," he said cautiously, "do we really need to take him? We are here for the healthy ones to help join the war. Why take the cripple?"

Amidst all the commotion, Hermann's head hung down to stare at the ground. He looked defeated and helpless.

"Yes, don't take him. Don't!" Both Hans and Karl were pleading. "We know what Hitler thinks about the handicapped!"

"Albert," Karl looked straight at their former friend. "You played soccer with us. Hermann was our goalie, and a good one. He is your neighbor. Who knows what will happen to him in a home? Please don't. Please!" He stretched out his arms in front of Hermann, trying to shield him.

In a sudden fit of rage, Albert ripped the Karabiner 43 rifle off his shoulder and aimed it the boys. The frown lines above his dark brown eyes had narrowed. "You two get dressed quickly or else!" he shouted.

Turning to Ferdinand, the soldier who had dared counter him, he hissed, "We have orders! You know what Hitler thinks about this kind of waste of a person."

Hands held above their heads, Hans and Karl felt their faces go pale as the blood drained from them. They were infuriated by the way Albert had threatened them, and dared to talk like that about their brother! But with the rifle pointed at them, they knew there was little they could do.

What would happen to Hermann? They dreaded the answer.

Ferdinand reluctantly turned away from Albert, and as if just remembering that he was the lower ranked SS officer, he dejectedly conceded, "Heil Hitler, your word is my order."

Both Hans and Karl took a few steps backwards, their hands held above their heads with Albert's rifle still aimed at them. They backed away from it until they hit the wall on the other side of Hermann's room, not once losing eye contact with the SS. Albert slowly lowered his weapon down to his side.

"This is no joke!" he seethed.

Hans and Karl lightly exhaled. Albert had always been a sore loser with a scary hair-trigger temper. But it had been curtailed once more. "Don't worry about packing anything besides your Hitler Youth uniform, and bring some underwear and socks—the *Wehrmacht* will provide the rest. We don't have all night! *Schnell*! *Schnell*!" Albert now rushed them along.

As fast as they could move, Karl and Hans opened the top drawer of their shared dresser, pulling out sweaters. "No, you don't need that!" Ferdinand ordered as he slammed the drawer shut. "Only your Hitler Youth uniforms!"

The boys moved to the middle drawer to pull out their freshly pressed Hitler Youth uniforms in the middle drawer, as well as the dark blue woolen caps with the visor and a Hitler Youth pin on the front. The sides of the cap were buckled in front in an upward position and could be pulled down over the ears. They also grabbed their dark blue woolen trousers and the matching three-button pullovers, their black polished shoes, and their Hitler Youth arm patches.

"You won't need the patches!" Ferdinand commanded again.

The boys got dressed in their uniforms as fast as they could under the watch of the two soldiers.

Mutter tried to intervene again, but Hans quieted her.

"Mutter, stop, it's useless!" He walked to where she stood outside Hermann's room and tried to calm her.

"Frau Elheusch, *nein,* stay out! This is Fuehrer business. You are not to get involved!" Ferdinand said. "Your sons will be serving the Fuehrer—it's the best for the Vaterland. You should be very proud of them! And Hermann will be in good hands!" Hans thought he noticed a slight sadness crossing Ferdinand's face.

"Nooooooo!" she shrieked. The sound reminded Karl of the screeching pigs he had heard at his butcher shop often right before they got slaughtered.

"Mutter, we'll be alright," he tried to soothe, unconvincingly. Now dressed, he tried to console her, hugging her tightly.

As he held her, Karl whispered as softly as he could to calm her: "It's alright, Mutter. We are fine. We will be fine, I promise you, Hermann will be fine. They are armed. There is nothing we can do. Please control yourself, Mutter. It will all be all right if we just do what they say!"

Hans joined Mutter and Karl in their embrace, leaning in and wrapping his arms around both of them. "Karl is right," he said. "Hermann will be fine. Don't cry! We'll be back before you know it. You have to stay strong for us. You have to keep the store running, and you have to help Opa get the desk finished. It's so close to being done." It took all his inner strength to get these last words out while holding back tears.

"Enough of that. *Schnell!* Let's go. We don't have much time!" Impatiently Albert grabbed Hans's arm away from his mother. With his other hand, he also grabbed Karl's sleeve and yanked him ahead of both of them.

"Alright, alright, we are going. You don't have to push us," Karl pulled his arm away from Albert, and straightened out his sleeves as they were rushed down the steps.

"Stay down here, we will get Hermann," Albert ordered and marched back upstairs to Hermann's room. "Get dressed, Hermann. We are taking you to a home!"

"No! I am not going to a home!" Hermann responded defiantly.

"Please don't take him. He is fine here. He can't help your war. He is no use to you. Please, please, not Hermann, too," pleaded Mutter again, as she repeatedly tried to enter the room. But Ferdinand blocked the doorway.

"Frau Elheusch, enough of that! Hermann is coming with us. Those are our orders! Help Hermann get dressed or step aside!" Albert demanded.

"Mutter, let it be." Hans and Karl had come back up to support Hermann, but now were worried for her safety, knowing armed Albert's unpredictable temper. Hans grabbed Mutter by the shoulder and gently guided her to the side.

"I can help!" Karl offered. He stepped cautiously into Hermann's room with his hands up, so as not to startle the two soldiers while carefully gauging their reaction. They reluctantly allowed Karl to help with his brother—something he did every day.

Karl helped Hermann sit up while Mutter now also eagerly jumped in to get Hermann's clothes. They somberly and quietly dressed him, with Hermann doing his part to help. Only their mother's sniffles could be heard.

After Hermann was dressed, Karl and Hans grabbed him under his knees to lift him up in a well-practiced routine and carried him downstairs.

"Take that wheelchair, Albert," Karl ordered the SS, pointing to where it sat beside the stairwell. Albert had helped with the wheelchair many times before when they were playmates.

The SS soldier unfolded the rusty wheelchair and rolled it to the bottom of the staircase so the two brothers could place Hermann into it.

"Let me grab your coat, Hermann." Mutter rushed to the coat closet to grab his winter coat and a hand-knit black scarf. She hastily put the coat on Hermann and then lovingly wrapped the scarf around his neck. As she buttoned up the coat and tucked in his scarf, her eyes again filled with tears. "You take good care of yourself." She kissed Hermann's forehead, then hugged him tightly. Hans and Karl looked on helplessly.

Hermann also knew what Hitler thought about the handicapped: that they were a burden to society and didn't deserve to live. He began to shiver as the reality of what was happening set in.

"Enough of that; we need to go!" Albert demanded impatiently. "Hans and Karl, you are coming with me. Ferdinand will take Hermann to the home."

He opened the front door and pushed Hans and Karl in front of him, with Ferdinand wheeling Hermann behind them. Then in a fleeting moment of respect to her, both of the soldiers stopped to click their heels one last time, stretched out their arms to salute, and said "Heil

Hitler" in unison to Mutter. She stood there helplessly and watched them take her three sons that night, not knowing whether she would ever see them again.

****

"The captain has turned on the seatbelt signs, we'll be landing in Washington, DC in approximately twenty minutes,"

Karl hears the welcomed announcement crackling through the old speakers. What relief he feels, after the longest flight he had ever taken: eight hours and thirty minutes from Germany to Dulles Airport. After a bumpy descent with seemingly never-ending turning maneuvers along with the loud engine's roar with its incessant accelerating and decelerating, the wheels finally touch down hard. Karl is pushed back into his seat while the airplane brakes work intensely to slow the taxiing plane. He presses his fingertips against his ears to muffle out the screaming noise until finally the plane comes to a near stop.

As it continues to roll to its final destination, Karl leans back and closes his eyes:

I will see Ellie in a few minutes.

He exhales. He made it. He feels rather weak, but he has made it.

This first trip to the U.S. has special meaning to him. His thoughts drift temporarily to his life during WWII and the time he spent with the American GIs nearly sixty years ago.

"Excuse me!" The plane has now stopped, and Karl's seatmate is trying to get around Karl to get to his luggage. Karl moves slowly as he feels the excitement of everyone around him wanting to get off. Standing impatiently in the aisle behind him a little boy about four years old is holding a red ball in one hand; in his other, he is holding a young, tired-looking woman's. The woman is wearing a beautiful grey woolen suit with immaculately placed black buttons. It is perfectly tailored, and the material looks exquisite.

Karl then notices the elderly woman standing in the isle with her small suitcase in front of her. *Who am I calling elderly, she is probably my age*, Karl chuckles to himself.

He wishes he has some flowers or something to hand to his daughter when he sees her now after all this time, but the simple wooden jewelry box he had hand-carved for her would have to make do. He's always kept a tulip garden at the family home in Germany. Red tulips were his favorite, even though he grew them in almost any color imaginable—even multicolored. But years ago he had to give up gardening, as it had become too hard on his aging knees.

How did I let five years pass by without seeing her? Ellie had visited Germany for two weeks back then, and now he had put himself through the ordeal of this long overseas flight. How quickly the time had passed by. He shakes his head quietly.

At age forty, Karl had his first heart attack. The doctor had warned him to stop smoking or else. And he had instantly stopped his habit of smoking two-packs of HBs a day. Of course he still remembers the cigarette brand; he had often had Ellie fetch a package for him at the cigarette machine installed in front of his brother-in-law's house across the street.

But he stopped after the attack. It had really scared everyone, and he realized surviving it was yet another chance at life. He has been having heart issues ever since.

For the past ten years, Ellie and Karl have called each other almost every weekend. Eventually, Ellie had convinced him to buy a computer, and taught him how to use the then barely-known free phone service Skype, so they could avoid the large overseas phone bills of the past.

They have also stayed in touch writing letters, though she does not write as many as she used to. Sometimes she sends him his favorite chocolate—"Hershey's"—because it's more difficult to get where he lives. She knows his story of why he specifically likes the Hershey's chocolate brand more than the many other German ones.

Ellie initially came to the DC area during a summer to take a few college courses at one of the local universities. She told Karl then how she had immediately fallen in love with the hardworking people, inventive attitudes and the bustling culture—the monuments, endless museums, theaters, and sports games. Then there were also the surrounding lakes and hiking paths that appealed to her love of the outdoors. The DC area offerings were so much broader than her village upbringing.

A company eventually sponsored her work visa and supported her through all the immigration and visa paperwork. In 1995, Karl's daughter had become a U.S. citizen, and she has been living in Northern Virginia all of her adult life.

He is in deep thought when his turn comes to step into the isle to get off the plane. The passenger behind him impatiently pushes him along.

Karl gets through customs quickly and walks through the long corridors to the shuttle that will take him to the welcome gate. A tall, blond, handsome man in his thirties stands there with three balloons. "Dad!" Karl hears the little red ball boy's high-pitched scream, and watches as the boy loosens his grip from the woman in the woolen grey suit and darts toward the man with open arms. He drops his ball. "Dad!" the boy screams again and flies into the arms of his father, who is now crouched down to scoop up his little boy.

Karl fleetingly wonders how long the boy's dad has been gone. The little family looks so happy to see each other again.

A slew of teenagers dressed in matching soccer uniforms, energetically joking and laughing with each other, showing their colorful braces, is bouncing past him.

A few middle-aged women who have been expressively chatting with each other now turn toward the teens, followed by a noisy welcome with energetic hugging and laughing.

The woman in the grey suit follows her husband, the abandoned red ball now tucked under her arm, with their son beaming tightly in his arms. She hands his luggage to a driver as they disappear into the crowd.

Karl looks away from the welcome spectacles, and scans the crowd again for his Ellie. He finally picks her out of the crowd, and his wrinkled face turns into an enormous smile. She is running toward him with open arms, overjoyed. "Papa!" she screams. For a second, he feels as thrilled as that little boy with the red ball. For a second, she is his little girl again.

Stopping his cart loaded with two large brown suitcases, he waits for her with his own arms held open. They squeeze each other tightly, almost crushing the tulips she is holding in her hands. She quickly hands them to him, and as one of the tulip petals falls onto the cold airport floor, tears of happiness well in his eyes.

"Oh, red tulips!" he says, as he admires them. Then he looks at her. "You haven't changed a bit!"

Ellie studies him, glancing at him sideways. "Your teeth look different!"

He laughs. His middle daughter has never missed the slightest change. Even as a kid, she noticed even his touch-up haircuts or the slightest change in his facial expressions. She was always able to gauge his moods; and there definitely had been a cadre of mood swings, given his undiagnosed PTSD from the war. He knows that being raised by a Hitler Youth-educated man has not always been easy for her.

"Yes," he says. "I had two dental implants put in here in the front." He points to his top front teeth. Forgetting for a minute that he is feeling weak, Karl is beaming, happy to see his daughter after all these years. He continues to evaluate her. She looks happy, so grown up and sophisticated in her matching white blouse and black skirt with black pumps. Her soft, childlike features have sharpened.

Suddenly Karl catches sight of a Jewish man, distinguished by his Kippah, walking by. He flinches ever so slightly, as if he wants to duck and hide in shame. No matter how much time has passed, his time in World War II, even only at sixteen years of age, has stayed with him.

"How was the flight?" Ellie asks, pulling Karl back to the present.

"The food was okay. You know I am very picky." Only the food grown from his garden and generally his own cooking was the best.

"Hopefully it wasn't too fatty?" She has always been concerned for his health.

A shadow falls over his face. His heart had been bothering him more during the flight than he wanted to admit. His pulse at times was too low for him to detect, and he had dull chest pains. Now he is out of breath just pushing the suitcases. But he says nothing. He doesn't want to worry Ellie.

"Here let me get that," she says as she grabs the handles from him to push the cart. He relinquishes control without any complaints.

"What's the matter, Dad?"

"Ah, nothing much, you know my old heart." He pauses and hesitates to say more.

"Are you in pain?" She asks, not bothering to hide her worry.

"No, just my heart...the usual." He brushes off her concerns as he tries to catch his breath.

"Dad, what is it? Just tell me what's wrong!" Ellie demands. Karl can hear the impatience in her voice.

"Well, my heart. It was bothering me during this flight."

"I am dialing 911."

"Nope!" Karl grabs for Ellie's phone. "Don't! I am fine!"

"No, you need to go to the hospital!"

"No, it's okay! This is not new; it all started at home," He is speaking slowly now, with a lowered voice and labored breathing. "I picked up a prescription on Friday. So, it's only been a few days since I started taking this new medication. Maybe it's just now kicking in, having this strange effect. And the flight probably worsened things. You know the air in those cabins is so thin, sometimes I feel I can't breathe up there."

Ellie is not convinced. "Okay, let's sit down over here at this coffee shop," she suggests. "Let me feel your pulse."

Hooking her right arm under her father's, she struggles with her left hand to push his cart filled with the heavy suitcases to the nearest empty table at the coffee shop. She then grabs Karl's hand to help him sit down. She wraps her two fingers and thumb around his wrist to feel his pulse and compares it to the seconds ticking along on her phone's timer.

"Dad, your pulse does seem slow!" Her concern rises, and she begins to scold him.

"You probably shouldn't have taken this long overseas flight. I warned you about that. I was worried about your heart. You just now got new heart medication, too? Did your doctor even say it's OK for you to fly? Remember, we talked about you getting her approval."

"Since when do I need to ask a doctor whether I can come see my daughter?" Karl laughs weakly in an attempt to joke. "But yes, I told Dr. Magdalene that I am coming to see you, and she didn't say I couldn't."

Dr. Magdalene was the small-town family doctor who had treated him since his first heart attack. She had also treated Ellie when she was a child.

"Dad, you don't look too good," Ellie insists. "Let me at least call a doctor."

"No, let's just sit here a bit longer. I just need to take a break," Karl declines weakly through his labored breathing. "I'll be fine." He tries to reassure her as he sits slouched in the uncomfortable coffee shop chairs. "Please get me a glass of water. That always makes me feel better."

"Papa, I can get you water, but I really think you need an ambulance?" Ellie insists.

Karl refuses. "Don't exaggerate, Ellie. I don't need an ambulance. I'll be fine if I just sit here for a bit. The flight was just exhausting for your old father."

Ellie studies him, calming down a bit. She orders a glass of water without ice at the counter and brings it over. "Here, drink this all up."

Watching him gulp the water, she suggests, "Papa, maybe I can get you a wheelchair to get you out of this airport?"

Then without waiting for a reply, she gets up. "You stay right here. I'll get you a wheelchair so I can wheel you to my car, and then I want to bring you to one of the best cardiologists in the area. I'll find you one here in Georgetown. Only the best doctor for you," Ellie insists.

"No," Karl refuses. "I don't need to see a doctor. Bring me to your house. I just need to rest; I'll be fine."

"Dad, this is not the time to be stubborn!"

Chapter 2

The Doctor's Visit

Dr. Schlesinger's graduate degree and her other medical accomplishments are lined up perfectly in dark brown wooden frames, covering almost every inch of her white office walls.

The blood pressure cuffs are tightly gripping Karl's upper arm. Exhausted, he is once again slouched sideways in an uncomfortable wooden chair. This time, in the Georgetown doctor's small office.

"90 over 48," says the nurse.

Karl doesn't speak any English and the little he had learned from the GIs so many decades ago he has mostly forgotten. Ellie translates for him, and he knows that it is low, especially in light of his normally high blood pressure.

"I'll get a glass of water," Dr. Schlesinger's assistant, Michelle, offers.

Ellie had called Dr. Schlesinger's number from the airport. She had told Karl on the way that her co-worker Janice had been praising the cardiologist for months, ever since Janice's mom had heart bypass surgery. Within weeks her mother was almost back to her normal self, and Janice credited Dr. Schlesinger's outstanding expertise. Ellie had always thought in the back of her mind that her dad could benefit from seeing this doctor, and she had wondered how she could get him to come here, given he was a world away. But she never brought it up—she knew he would not travel this far to see a cardiologist.

Now here Karl was, sitting in her office much sooner than Ellie could have anticipated.

Dr. Schlesinger walks in. A woman in her late thirties with shoulder-length brown locks elegantly framing her face. Ellie translates for her during the entire visit.

After introducing herself and her dad, Ellie quickly fills in the doctor.

Karl feels helpless not speaking the language. This is hardly how he had envisioned this trip at all. Here he was a continent away from home, in Washington, DC, with plans to visit his daughter for only a few weeks, and his first day is being spent in a cardiologist's office.

"He thinks his new medication is causing the issue. His doctor prescribed it recently," Ellie is saying.

"Does he have it with him?" Dr. Schlesinger asks.

Karl pulls out a plastic sandwich bag with various colors of medication containers in it. "Sure, it's right here."

He pulls out a brown bottle and hands it to the doctor. She inspects the name typed on the side of it.

"I know this medication. We will need to do a thorough check-up first, before I can tell whether it could be causing the problem. Please tell your dad that we'll do an EKG now and we'll continue to monitor his blood pressure during the EKG. You can wait here."

Ellie continues to translate for Karl, so he knows what to expect next, and then one of the assistants wheels Karl to the room next door.

"Please come and get me if you need anything translated," Ellie calls after the assistant.

After fifteen minutes, which seems more like an hour to Karl, Dr. Schlesinger calls Ellie into the check-up room where he is lying on the exam table, covered in a gown.

"The EKG shows some irregularities," the doctor says. "I want to give him a heart echocardiogram to get an even more detailed picture. If that's okay with him. Can you ask him to give his approval?"

Ellie translates, telling Karl it's only for the best, and this time he approves quickly. Dr. Schlesinger's trustworthy demeanor seems to be calming him.

The assistant rolls in the heart echocardiogram machine and she hooks Karl up to it, while Ellie is watching from only a few feet away.

"Dad, should I wait outside?" she asks, not wanting to intrude on his privacy.

"No, no, please stay," he insists. "I need you to translate. Also, I don't want to be alone in here."

Dr. Schlesinger waves her to come closer. "I'd like to show you something. Please translate for your father. Pull up closer." She points to the empty chair sitting at the end of the room.

Pulling up the chair to the desk, Ellie tries to focus on the screen with a gray mass displayed on the monitor that Dr. Schlesinger is pointing to.

With both Karl and Ellie looking on, Dr. Schlesinger motions to an area of the screen: "Here the blood flow is very good; you can see the regular heartbeat, resulting in high blood flow." She points to the area where the heart is pulsating regularly, and the mass is full. Then she moves to point at the outer edge of the heart, to the area that's flatter than the rest of the mass.

"See this? This is what's called an enlarged area of the heart, and here hardly any blood is flowing through. You can barely see the heart pulsating. The area here is much flatter, and it appears somehow his heart has been damaged in this area." Karl and Ellie can both clearly see the difference between the mass of the pulsating heart area and the thinner outlying area.

"Also, a healthy heart size ends around here," Dr. Schlesinger continues, while motioning to the edge of three-quarters of the heart. "Your dad's heart is enlarged."

Karl starts to feel nauseated seeing his heart displayed on a monitor while having to listen to all the problems with it. Although he cannot understand the words, he can see what the doc was pointing to and notices the concern on both hers and Ellie's faces. Can his heart issues be fixed? He has so many questions, but then Ellie translates, repeating the same pointing motions on the monitor and explaining what she was told.

Dr. Schlesinger continues her diagnosis. "It could be that your dad had a cold or some type of viral infection, and this enlargement is the by-product of it. Or," she hesitates, "it could be from too much alcohol. Did your dad drink a lot when he was younger, or is he still a heavy drinker now?"

"No," Ellie assures the doctor without asking her dad. "Drinking is not an issue now." When Karl was much younger, before he was even married, he had his share of beer, schnapps, and drunken episodes, but drinking hadn't been and wasn't an issue since he got married.

"It must be caused by an infection, the flu perhaps or a cold," she insists.

Nevertheless, she reluctantly translates the question—and her immediate answer—to her dad, and he confirms, "No, I really don't drink much at all. A glass of wine here or there, but that's it." Then, seeking reassurance, he adds, "A glass of red wine here and there is even supposed to be healthy, isn't it?"

But Ellie has turned back to the doctor. "What does this mean? Does he need surgery? Heart-bypass surgery? What do you think needs to be done for him? What is needed for an enlarged heart?" As her questions just pour out, Karl notices that she is not trying to conceal her worry any longer. "Is this a common heart problem?"

Her anxiety is obvious to everyone in the room. Karl wants to walk over to calm her down, but is too weak to move.

Dr. Schlesinger tilts her head and says, "He needs a stent to his heart. That will support the artery leading to the unhealthy portion. I also have to put him on different blood thinners. I need to adjust his medication, and he should then be as good as new."

She smiles in a warm, calming manner before she continues.

"The medication he is on right now is absolutely the wrong kind. I would never prescribe that type of medication for your dad's current condition. It slows down the heartbeat even further. This might have been useful for some of his other heart issues in the past, but I suggest he stops taking it."

Because she is not his doctor, Dr. Schlesinger says she can only prescribe a mild version of the medication she thinks he actually needs

"If you all approve," she says, "I will write a prescription now."

"I also recommend we keep him in the hospital overnight to monitor how he reacts to the new prescription," she continues. "I can put the stent in within a week. But that will require a hospital stay, and I am not sure his insurance will cover it."

Karl wants to know what was going on. As Ellie translates, Karl starts to feel angry at his house doctor, Dr. Magdalena. How could she prescribe the wrong medication? She never did a heart echocardiogram, and simply prescribed the same medication or different variations of it. Karl doubts she would even have the heart echocardiogram equipment in her small-town family practice. But even if she didn't have it, Dr. Magdalena could have referred him to a doctor in the city who had the equipment.

He listens to what Ellie says the doctor told her, and before Ellie has even finished translating, Karl interrupts her. "No way, Ellie. I will not have surgery here in the U.S. It's completely out of the question!"

Ellie turns to repeat her dad's decision to Dr. Schlesinger.

The doctor nods. "Then I recommend he fly back home as soon as possible to see his doctor. Though it will be at his own risk—your dad needs to have that surgery as soon as possible, and with this specific dose I am giving him, he needs to be monitored closely until we are sure it's the right dose. I will write up a report and recommendations that your dad can give to his doctors to follow up."

"Sounds good!" Ellie replies. "Is it safe to bring my dad back to my house overnight, until we can get him a flight back?"

Dr. Schlesinger shakes her head vehemently. "Sorry, no. Like I said, I highly recommend he spend the night at the hospital where he can be monitored. We can't exactly predict his reaction to this medication. At least in the hospital, if his condition worsens, someone will be right there to help."

As Dr. Schlesinger writes up the instructions for Karl to take back home to Dr. Magdalena, which she will need to follow those closely, Ellie turns back to Karl.

"You are going to the hospital for at least one night," she orders. Her tone tells Karl that she is not asking for his permission this time.

"I'll get you on a flight back as quickly as possible," she continues. "I will also call your insurance. And please, don't see Dr. Magdalena when you go back. Please go straight to the hospital in Nürnberg. They will have better facilities and better equipment, and the doctors there will have the most recent up-to-date education. Just like Dr. Schlesinger here."

Ellie also informs Karl that Dr. Schlesinger thinks that Dr. Magdalena prescribed the wrong type of medication, and asks if she had ever run a heart echocardiogram on him.

As Ellie suspected, her dad answers no. He has never seen such state-of-the-art equipment.

A knock on the door interrupts the intimate check-up and discussions, and the office assistant sticks her head half-in, as if too embarrassed to walk in. "I am sorry, Ms. Elheusch, but we can't accept the German health insurance you provided us."

Ellie is not surprised. "Can I write a check? When my dad is back in Germany, he can file the claim with his insurance. He has international health insurance."

Dr. Schlesinger stops the assistant before she leaves. "Don't charge them for the heart echocardiogram," she instructs. "That would be $1,500 by itself. Only bill them for the EKG and the general office visit."

Ellie is taken aback by the unexpected kindness and immediately translates for her dad, who also is aghast at Dr. Schlesinger's generosity. "Not sure we can accept that, Ellie!"

"It's okay, Dad. If she doesn't want to bill us for it, just accept it gracefully."

Karl turns to Dr. Schlesinger, sticking out his hand. "Sank you, Sank you," he says, repeating one of the few English expressions he actually is able to repeat in his heavy German accent.

Dr. Schlesinger responds, "Oh, don't worry about it at all. My dad is originally from Southern Germany. He came here in 1946."

"Yes, Schlesinger is a very common German last name," Ellie says.

"That's actually my married name. My husband also has German ancestry—I am surrounded by Germans. But I regret that I never really learned the language. I know bits and pieces, but am far from fluent." She attempts a tired smile.

Karl finds her story fascinating. "Ask her where her dad is from in Southern Germany, or if she knows whether any of her relatives still live in Germany?" He is getting his energy back now that he knows the adjusted medication should make him feel better.

But not understanding him, Dr. Schlesinger quickly instructs the assistant, "Mary, call an ambulance and make all the necessary arrangements. Let's send him to Fairfax Hospital for the night, so he can be monitored there."

Ellie translates the plans to Karl. He tries one more weak attempt at protesting but soon realizes this decision has been made.

After what seems forever, the ambulance arrives. Ellie is allowed to sit in the back with Karl on his way to the hospital. Once he is checked in and resting comfortably, Ellie decides to stay the night in the room with him.

"No, Ellie, you go home and get a good night's rest. I am fine here; I am in good hands."

But she insists she will stay, and that is the final word. Before too long, the lengthy overseas trip catches up with Karl, and he falls into a deep slumber.

Chapter 3

Background

Karl was six years old when Hitler became Chancellor of Germany in 1934. Four years later, when Karl turned ten, his school required he to become a member of an organization called the German Young People. At fourteen, he was then required to join the Hitler Youth. As with all boys aged fourteen to eighteen years old, he and his brother, Hans, didn't have any choice other than to join and attend.

The three brothers—Karl, Hans, and Hermann—lived with their mother in their grandpa's house in a small village, nestled in the hills and valleys at the outskirts of Nuremberg. Curly, red-haired and green-eyed, Karl was the youngest and fairest of the three teenagers, each two years apart. His older brother Hans' hair was blonder, his eyes blue and his skin redder. Hermann, the oldest at nineteen, had red hair with freckles covering his forehead and nose, and used a wheelchair to get around. Hermann kept his hair long. It was his way to rebel, much to the dismay of his mother. But Opa, his grandfather, convinced her that there were worse things a boy could be doing.

For the longest time, Karl's family had tried to figure out why Hermann wasn't strong enough to hold himself up and walk on his own. Mutter had desperately gone from doctor to doctor seeking a cure for her son. But given the poor state of medicine in 1930s Germany, they eventually came to grips with the fact that Hermann would have to use a wheelchair. Religious Opa often wondered whether it was a punishment from God, and Herman's mother was inclined to believe him. It wasn't until much later, after the war, that

Hermann would be diagnosed with muscular dystrophy. Because of his condition, he was categorized as a cripple and excused from the Hitler Youth.

The boys' father had died in a moped accident when Karl was only eight months old. It had been a gruesome accident. Mutter had arrived at the scene to witness her husband lying in the road with his severed leg lying tangential to his body in the middle of the street, blood everywhere. His moped had been hit by a speeding driver who cut a curve too short, instantly killing Karl Sr. and dragging his body for a while.

After seeing the severed leg and her husband's body, Mutter refused to get near him and remained at a distance watching the spectacle of people trying to revive him. She just stood there helpless and distraught until his body was taken away. Eventually, Frau Müller, a neighbor, wrapped her arm around Mutter and walked her home. Opa had to make the funeral arrangements. From then on, living with Opa was the only solution for the small family as they would have struggled on their own. Three years into the war, food was scarce, and the store shelves were mostly empty. Three generations living together had become very common.

Karl knew his dad from a few old black-and-white pictures, but mostly from the comforting stories Mutter would tell. His dad had been a hard worker, and for his multitude of services was a well-liked man in the county. Secretly, Karl often yearned for him—especially before the war, when he saw the neighborhood kids playing with their dads; or even just when he watched his friends interact with their fathers, their arms wrapped around each other or holding each other's hands. But Karl learned early on to control his emotions and feelings; he knew telling Mutter about how much he missed having a father would make her upset. When all of his friends' dads were later recruited, he no longer felt as inadequate in comparison. He and his friends now shared the common bond of being fatherless.

Opa ran his own carpentry business out of the house. Years ago, Karl's great-grandfather had turned the basement level of his modest brick-house into a carpentry shop. It had a separate downstairs entrance, and still hanging in front of it was the original sign used by the great-grandfather, distinguished by the old symbols of the carpentry guild: a carpenter's plane, a square and a compass.

The carpentry connected to a large back storage room and housed an assortment of wood and tools: one hand-drill, three axes, two saws, three chisels, two squares, one level, one wrench, a large dresser filled with all types of nails, screws, screwdrivers and hammers, and a variety of paint sitting beside it, along with any other wood supply one could think of.

Karl's maternal uncle, Joseph, had helped out in the family's carpentry business until October 1939, when Joseph was ordered to join the war. One rainy morning, a caravan of *Wehrmacht* trucks idled outside in the streets, standing ready for the new recruits. Along with their neighbors, relatives and friends, Opa, Mutter, Karl, Hans, and Hermann in his wheelchair, all stood outside in the drizzle, looking on helplessly as Uncle Joseph disappeared with others into the back of the trucks. Then together they waved their sad and destitute goodbyes as the truck caravan disappeared past the horizon.

They hadn't heard from Uncle Joseph since that unforgettable autumn morning. Too many times to count, Mutter inquired about any type of news of her brother at the local *Gruppenhaus,* the makeshift city hall. But to no avail. She was told over and over not to worry, that everything was all right, and that if anything were wrong, she would have heard.

But everyone knew that something had to be wrong. They hadn't heard from Uncle Joseph at all.

The flamboyant neighbor living diagonally across the street, Frau Müller, received two letters from her husband, each one a year apart, providing her with renewed hope. He was fighting at the Russian front in Moscow, he said, and he hoped to be back soon. Hauptmann Müller had been recruited the same day as Uncle Joseph, and Mutter had asked Frau Müller if her husband had mentioned anything in the letters about her brother. But while Hauptmann Müller complained that he hadn't received any letters from his frau, even though she had sent at least twenty letters to him, there was no mention of Uncle Joseph.

What had become of Uncle Joseph, and all those letters Frau Müller had sent? Why was her husband not receiving them? Frau Müller also inquired at the local city hall, but that day she was told to "consider herself lucky if they don't stop by with other news", which she considered so heartless that she vowed to never return there again. She continued to write the letters but asked a friend of hers to drop them off at the city hall in hopes that one of the letters would make it to her dearly missed husband. She never heard from him again, and questions about Uncle Joseph's whereabouts were never answered. Yet the Müller and Elheusch families never gave up hope…

Karl and Hans filled in as the breadwinners for their father and uncle. Their circumstances had forced them to mature early.

The family relied on Hans herding the neighbors' cows, and they also at times shared some of their modest potato harvest in exchange for the farmer's eggs, flour or other small items. Most stores couldn't keep daily staples in stock.

They would borrow the farmer's plow horse each spring to dig the furrows on the small field they owned, located next to Opa's house, so the boys together with Mutter could plant the potatoes evenly-spaced. Continuously they would water and weed the small field, watching the green sprouts grow with excitement, and a few months later they would harvest their modest crop. All the bending was tiring, yet it was fulfilling work, because they knew the bounty would feed them for a few months or they could use it for trade.

The furniture they built or repaired out of Opa's carpentry, mostly for neighbors, provided them with an additional income during these hard times, whether the payment came in the form of currency or other supplies.

Karl had found his passion early on while tinkering with wood in Opa's carpentry. For him, carpentry was nearly an art: he enjoyed the sawing, measuring, chiseling, and refinishing of the wood to create a final and unique product. Whether it was building a dresser drawer, repairing the roof of a neighbor's house, or fixing a window frame, he could do it all.

Under the direction of Opa and Mutter, Karl quickly became very proficient in wood-working. And while he eagerly did all the necessary work, Karl took more of a liking to carpentry than Hans did to herding. Karl viewed the hard labor associated with chopping the trees, shaving the tree trunks and then cutting them to size as necessary up-front work to gather the needed material to build and create the furniture.

He was following in the footsteps of proud carpenters. The carpentry of the Elheusch family was already well known in the area from decades of quality work. Word of their fine craft continued to spread. Customers and even non-customers in their small village became aware of the unique furniture that Opa, Mutter, and then Karl were crafting.

Karl's dream was to earn the official title of carpenter someday, with a certificate to back it up, like Opa's or his father's whose hung on the white carpentry walls. Opa at one point had thought to remove Karl Sr.'s certificate, but Mutter had insisted it remain.

Karl would need to take additional carpentry classes and become an apprentice in the neighboring city's carpentry shop for a couple of years before getting this final "Schreiner Meister" master of carpentry certificate. But while he had started on it, there were many reasons Karl couldn't finish his apprenticeship right away.

Opa needed his help in the shop, and mostly, the Hitler Youth didn't allow for those plans. So in the meantime, Opa's continued "on the job" training would have to do.

Karl dropped out of school at the beginning of 8th grade, deciding that helping out in Opa's carpentry was much more important than listening to the propaganda he was being taught in school or at the Hitler Youth meetings. "Propaganda" was Mutter's most-used word those days for the falsities she insisted the Nazis were spreading to the naïve masses.

Mutter was adamantly opposed to everything that had to do with Hitler and the war. She knew from listening to the forbidden channels on her radio that the Allies were closing in and that too many lives were being lost daily. She had been against Hitler from the time she first heard anything about him, and she never bought into the Nazi ideology and the nationalistic belief it was spreading. She despised the censorship the Nazis imposed on her, like telling her which books she could read, or what could be written in the newspaper.

Mutter remained resentful of the regime and missed the days when she could listen to anything on the radio without censorship. Not that there were many *Volkssender* channels to choose from then—but there were no restrictions and no threats if one listened to any desired channel or read anything that was available. Now, Propaganda minister Joseph Goebbels would refer to the foreign media as the "Lying Press". According to the propaganda, everyone but the Nazis was lying.

Mutter was also a practicing Catholic, but only in the secrecy of her own home. Opa, too, was a very staunch Catholic, though church masses no longer took place. All the Catholic priests had vanished or stopped practicing. Opa was becoming more and more withdrawn, mostly just working in his small carpentry, the boys being the only highlight in his days.

Mutter and Opa were appalled at how the Jews were being treated, and everything they heard about them being singled out and blamed for felt wrong. It was absolutely not right to treat another religion that way.

There had been one Jewish family—the Morgenthau family—residing in their village, who owned a small jewelry shop. One day a sign was put in front of their store that read, *"Deutsche wehrt euch, kauft nicht von Juden"*. It was warning the Germans to defend themselves, and not buy from Jews. Then the store was shuttered and a "Closed" sign was hung, a huge Star of David painted on the storefront.

Mutter said that it all reminded her too much of all the stories Opa had told her about World War I—another futile war started by ill-advised German leadership. In 1914, the German army had invaded neutral Belgium and northern France, executing thousands of Belgian and French civilians. Opa had lost an eye in battle during World War I, and repeatedly told tales about the senselessness and cruelties of that war and the needless human sacrifices that came with it. He was against this second war and convinced his daughter and grandsons that it was just another worthless fight, started by this lunatic Hitler.

It was Hitler's propaganda feeding into the dissatisfaction of a largely unemployed population that led much of the German population to be smitten by Hitler, initially. Over and over, Hitler blamed the Jews for the strong sanctions following World War I and the subsequent decline of the German economy. Hitler ordered the autobahn construction before the war, leading to a rise in employment. Because he improved German lives, many considered him a hero.

But Hitler never missed a chance to blame the Jews for Germany's demise since WWI.

"Hitler knew what to do about the unemployment and fixed it, we can trust him; hence he must also be right about the Jewish problem," was the basic logic of many Germans suffering at that time.

But eventually, civilian factories were turned into defense mills, and war fighter construction machines. And then it was too late for the German population to affect change.

****

Together with other neighborhood kids, Karl and Hans used to play soccer in their backyard with Hermann as the goalie.

That was something Hermann could do—he could sit in the grass and let his body fall side to side, guarding the narrow makeshift goal, the imaginary posts marked by chunks of wood. Despite his handicap, Hermann had always been part of the group: Karl, Hans, Albert, Daniel and Martin. They raced each other in the neighborhood streets, and Hermann would be the one giving the signal to start and refereeing if the race was ever close. They ran through the wheat fields with Hermann looking out for any grownups. (Their races dismayed the farmers, who often complained to the parents to keep their kids out of the fields, because trampled wheat plants would be impossible to harvest.) The boys also often explored the nearby creek and woods just down the hill from their houses.

One day they were hiking along the creek at the bottom of the large hill just a mile from home, stopping to poke at the tadpoles with twigs, when Albert suddenly grabbed a frog, pulled out a pocket knife and cut off the frog's leg.

"Yum! Frog legs!" he exclaimed, laughing and proudly holding up the frog by one leg while stuffing the amputated raw frog's leg into his mouth. The rest of the frog's body wiggled in torture.

"That's just cruel, Albert." Karl tried to wrestle the pocketknife from Albert's hand to stop him from cutting up another frog. "If you are going to cut it up, kill it first!" he protested.

In their shuffle for the knife, Albert cut Karl's thigh, escaped his grip and laughed the most gloating laugh. "What are you going to do? You can't stop me," he teased, holding up the knife as he ran to look for more frogs.

Blood seeped through Karl's khaki pant leg from the cut as he tried to cover up the wound with his hand to stop the bleeding. Dejectedly, Karl turned to Daniel, nodding toward the hill. "Let's go back; let's not be associated with him."

"Wait!" Daniel screamed. Before Karl could respond, Daniel had leaped onto Albert's back, holding him tight around his neck. Albert's knife fell to the muddy ground.

"Kick him!" Daniel ordered Karl. "In the shins, hard!"

Albert was choking, no match for the tall, muscular Daniel. He tried to kick back with hands and feet, flailing helplessly. Daniel laughed a deep roar at Albert's feeble attempt to break free.

"You're not that tough anymore, are you?" he mocked.

With a hand still pressed against his wound, Karl dug the knife out of the mud. Then he turned to Daniel. "No, not worth it. Let him go," he said, and began his trek back home.

Daniel pushed Albert away so hard that the boy feel face down into the muddy creek bed, then he rushed to catch up to Karl.

In the distance, they could hear Albert scream after Daniel, "You Jewish pig, I will get you!"

Daniel and Karl both flinched. That hurt more than any punch. On any other day, at any other moment, Karl would have turned around and together with Daniel punched that "little coward", as Karl referred to him. He had heard these types of Jewish insults far too often lately. He couldn't stand hearing classmates and others in the community talk about and treat Jews as if they were any different from Protestants or Catholics.

They were exactly the same as before Hitler came to power, Karl thought. The Morgenthau's, for instance, had been respectable business people; everyone in Karl's village had enjoyed having the only jewelry store in town, and people had bought treasures there for many occasions through which many memories had been made. The Morgenthau's had not changed at all. Only everyone's view of them changed, under Hitler's influence.

How is it so easy for one person to change a large population's opinion of an entire culture and religion? Karl had often wondered together with Daniel.

Daniel had told Karl how people who used to greet his parents in the street, men taking their hats off when his mom walked by or women smiling big to say "hello"; now everyone looked down when they saw them coming. Oftentimes they even crossed the street and kept walking on the other side to avoid them. Daniel had confided in Karl about how much he was suffering under this new mistreatment. Karl desperately wished there was something he could do about it.

But that day, red-cheeked and upset, in too much pain with his leg steadily bleeding, Karl had headed straight home to Mutter.

Karl noticed out of the corner of his eye that Daniel had turned around at the sound of Albert's insults, contemplating going back, but Karl waved off the idea.

"That coward!" he seethed. "He had to wait to say it until we were in a safe distance! Keep going, he is not worth it!"

Daniel hesitated a moment longer. Then, with his head hanging, he continued to follow Karl home.

Karl and Daniel both knew that these days, Daniel, the Jewish kid, could not afford any shenanigans. And Albert was not to be trusted; who knew how he would embellish the story.

Karl downplayed the wound to Mutter as a result of accidentally cutting himself. Though suspicious, she was focused on taking Karl to the doctor, where he got stitches to close the deep gash. The doctor said that if the wound had been just a few millimeters farther right, it could have hit the femoral artery and been life-threatening.

Karl and Daniel both avoided Albert after that incident. They heard later from Hans that Albert was spreading rumors of "the Jewish pig" Daniel attacking him unprovoked, but Karl squelched those rumors immediately whenever given a chance. Albert was too much of a coward to face them directly.

****

Karl was fast asleep when the pebble colliding with his bedroom window made him jump right out of bed. He hastily opened the window and peered out, leaning over the painted white wooden sill, and discovered a shadow standing in the snow below it, motioning him to come down.

"Karl, hurry!"

Daniel's voice reflected an urgency Karl had never heard before. *What would Daniel need from him this late at night? Why did he sound so scared?*

Karl rushed down the steps, opened the front door quietly so as not to wake anyone, then slowly pulled it shut behind him to keep the cold winter air from coming in. The snow crunched under each step of his slippers as he walked to the back of the house to find Daniel.

"They arrested my dad!" the boy exclaimed as soon as he caught sight of Karl.

"What, who?"

"The SS came and got him!"

Karl stared at Daniel. "Why?"

"They just said they needed him to come to the town hall for questioning."

"But why?" Karl couldn't understand how they could just arrest Mr. Morgenthau without a reason.

"Don't you get it!" Daniel hissed impatiently, annoyed at his friend's naïve question. "It's because he is Jewish!"

Karl motioned for his upset friend to lower his voice. "Keep it down, we don't want to wake up Mutter or Opa!"

But Daniel was frantic. "Albert's father, SS Wüst, was leading the SS pack in the arrest. I think my sister Anna, Mom and I will be next!"

"No, they would have taken you also tonight if they wanted you." The look on Daniel's face immediately made Karl want to retract his statement. "You know what I mean," he attempted feebly. He was tired, standing out here on his backyard in this February night, the snow seeping into his slippers.

Daniel's mom, Frau Morgenthau, was a former Sommer. Because she was not Jewish, and only married to a Jewish man, there was a chance the SS might just leave her and her kids alone.

"Maybe they will let him go again after they are done questioning him?" Karl tried again, trying in vain to appease Daniel.

Daniel squinted back at Karl. "Has anyone come back after being taken in for questioning?" he hissed. "Your Catholic priest who was preaching against Hitler and disappeared? The teachers we haven't seen in years that refused to teach Nazi doctrine? And now my dad. We are next, Karl!"

Daniel looked down. The night shadows marking his face with what was looming.

Karl's brain worked feverishly to come up with a solution. But how could he help his friend? What could he do?

"Can you hide us?" Daniel begged.

This sudden request startled Karl from his thoughts. "What?! Where?"

"In your Opa's cellar," Daniel responded and then added quietly, "Mom asked me to ask you."

Karl looked at Daniel in disbelief. How could he and his mom make such a request? They knew how dangerous it would be for the Elheusch's to be caught hiding the only Jewish people in town.

"Everyone knows you and your family around here," Karl reasoned. "And how would we hide you? You know that others use the cellar as a bomb shelter."

Daniel looked down, defeated. But Karl could relate to the desperation and fear.

"Alright," Karl relented. "I'll ask Opa tomorrow." At the sight of the faint smile that crossed Daniel's face, he quickly added, "I really doubt he will agree to it."

He grabbed Daniel's shoulder tight. "I will let you know. But now I need some sleep. I have to get up early and help Opa. Good night."

The next day Karl replayed over and over in his head how he would best present Daniel's request to Mutter and Opa at dinner. He needed the right setting and mood to bring up such a "preposterous request", as he was sure Opa and Mutter would call it.

He would recommend that they could stack all the wood in their shed in such a way that the Morgenthaus would be well hidden, but still had room to move around. He would be responsible for feeding them, and he would dump their waste in their toilet, and they only could come out at night... So many things would have to fall into place.

He waited in anxious anticipation for dinner. When his family had finally gathered around the dinner table, Karl was well prepared to present the question with his solution. He now was adamant and was sure he could convince them of his plan.

They barely had sat down at the dinner table, and Mutter was especially outraged that day. "These poor kids! It's just horrible!" she exclaimed. Distraught, she went on to tell her sons and Opa about what she had heard on the radio, the *Volkssender*.

"Last week, three college students at Munich University tried to resist the Hitler regime."

She lowered her voice to a whisper, afraid to be heard through the brick walls of their house. "They passed around leaflets at their university to open people's eyes about Hitler," she went on. "They were a brother and sister team—Geschwister Scholl was their name—along with their friends.

Mutter shook her head. "Apparently, a janitor saw them dropping the leaflets and without hesitation snitched them out. The young students were swiftly prosecuted, and within a day executed. Their punishment is to serve as an example of what will happen to anyone who stands against the regime."

She sighed. "Those students were right to protest and hand out those leaflets!"

"But look at their punishment!" Opa interjected somberly. "It doesn't pay to be a hero!"

"Right. Your life is not worth it!" agreed Mutter, directing her glare at her sons sitting across from her at the dinner table, which was covered with the linen tablecloth.

Mutter was so cautious and protective of her brood and for example, had been continuously coming up with many excuses for her sons so they could avoid attending the required Hitler Youth meetings, rather than outright resisting the regime. It was more important that Karl focused on improving his carpentry skills, she would claim, and Hans' extra income was needed to sustain the family.

Karl was nervously tugging at the corners of the table cloth, realizing this story didn't help his case. Karl felt horrible for those Scholl siblings, but was also growing anxious to present Daniel's question. With Mutter still so worked up, he knew it wasn't the right time yet. Maybe in a few minutes, he thought, if he could change the subject for a bit to something more positive.

But what positive topic is there these days?

Suddenly there was a loud knock at the front door. Startled, everyone turned toward the door at the end of the foyer. Who could be here this late? Then, without waiting for an answer, skinny Albert Wüst forced the door open and stormed in.

"Good evening!" Albert bellowed, with his greasy brown hair sleeked to the side and pimples all over his face. He strutted forward into the kitchen. In his freshly-creased Hitler Youth uniform and high, shiny, black boots, he moved around as if it were his own home. He had been to their house many times when he was younger, when he and the Elheusch boys were still playing with each other, and he felt very comfortable here.

"I was sent here because Hans and Karl missed yet another meeting," he was saying. "As you all well know, all boys and girls have to attend all required meetings. It is the law—it went into effect March 1939!" He dramatically pointed his finger in the air to emphasize his point.

"Not only is it now required by law, but there are also many reasons and benefits. Your sons can't miss any more meetings, Frau Elheusch," Albert spoke directly to Mutter in his crackly, adolescent voice, staring hard at her.

His father was a leader in the *Schutzstaffel* (SS), and Albert was a stout follower of the Hitler Youth, rising quickly to a leadership rank. His strong belief in the Nazi ideology was clear. Karl had seen him mainly in his uniform, hardly ever in civilian clothes anymore. Karl had also seen him participating in all the marches that now so often took place through the small village, the streets lined in red flags with large swastikas on them.

Karl studied Albert's face as he continued his rant. Two years older, Albert had been one of Karl's playmates just a few years ago. Hans and Albert had been in the same grade. The knife incident last summer was only a little over a year ago, and that had been the last time Karl had had any contact with Albert. Since then, they had avoided each other.

Here, in their kitchen, in his overly-starched brown Hitler Youth uniform shirt and black pants, with the black swastika stitched on a white and red patch wrapped around his left arm, Albert was pacing back and forth, causing the old wooden kitchen floors in Opa's house to creak with every one of his strides. It was as though the wooden planks were complaining about his very presence. Albert continued to ramble off his demands.

"They cannot miss another meeting!"

This was nothing new. It was the same message Karl heard on Mutter's radio when she listened to the Nazi news: all youth were required to attend the Hitler Youth meetings.

Mutter had talked about all the brainwashed people in the past, and watching Albert now, Karl was convinced it was true.

Mutter knew that she would be held responsible for her sons' Hitler Youth attendance. Missing the meetings was a criminal offense, punishable by a fine of 150 marks or imprisonment. Karl and his brother had enjoyed being members of the Catholic Youth Club, and they resented the fact that after joining the Hitler Youth they were ordered to denounce their Catholic Youth membership. They no longer were allowed to take part in any religious activities, or else they would face serious punishment.

"The Hitler Youth law came into effect on March 25, 1939," Albert continued to rattle on, "and it includes the youth-service duty requirement. In the Hitler Youth, we will make sure the youths know the purpose of the Third *Reich*. All younger members are mentored and trained by the smarter, young adults who will help implement the goals of our Führer. They will help build the 'Thousand-year *Reich*'."

Karl watched his every move, listening to him carefully and reading every cue. *He is wasting his time here.* Karl was still convinced that Mutter would come up with the right explanations as to why they couldn't attend all the meetings. The carpentry and the cows need tending to.

After a while longer of attentively listening to Albert's rambling, Karl had grown increasingly impatient, and couldn't wait for Albert to leave. Mutter had made carrot soup with a few potatoes added to it; the pot of soup was sitting on the dining room table, and the steam that had been rising from it had now stopped. And after dinner, Karl still needed to help Hans clean out the carpentry as they had promised Opa.

He couldn't take it any longer. He stood and excused himself. "Sorry, I need to go. I have to clean the carpentry."

"No, you need to hear this!" Albert barked back so intensely he stopped Karl mid-movement. "*Especially* you! I see you still hanging out with that Jewish pig!"

There it was again… Karl despised that word.

"He is Jewish but he is not a pig," Karl replied through gritted teeth, his hand rolled into a fist.

"What is it with you and that Morgenthau? You as an Arian should really stay away from him! Aryans and Jews should not mingle. You need to be careful, Karl, they have arrested people for less than hanging out with a Jew."

Karl wanted to respond with "He used to be your friend too!" but realized there was no reasoning with Albert. No, he did not want to be arrested. Mutter would not survive losing another family member. Annoyed, Karl bit his tongue and slowly sat back down, glaring back at Albert. *Who does this guy think he is, just because he is in this uniform? What is it with the Nazis and Jews? Why can't they leave them alone?*

"I need to know that you will attend all the meetings. Nothing is more important than supporting the goal of our Führer. We need everyone's help, whether twelve years old or sixty. Promise me that you won't miss another meeting. Promise!" Albert lowered the passion that had risen in his voice. Leaning in close to be on eye level with Mutter, he paused for a split second before whispering emphatically, "…because I don't want to have to turn you all in."

Karl looked at Mutter, who seemed to have turned paler. A very weary look crossed her face. He stepped forward reflexively, trying to defend Mutter, aghast that Albert had just threatened her like that. But she quickly motioned Karl to stay back. Then slowly, she got up and held Albert's gaze, annunciating every word she directed at him.

"I have known you since the day you were born. I babysat you and even changed your diapers, and your mom, in turn, has watched Hans, Karl, and Hermann. You have played together, and you have eaten many meals here. And today you are here to threaten me?" Her voice ended in a higher pitch.

Albert looked away for a moment, digesting what he just heard before turning and staring back directly at Mutter, holding her gaze, resolved and sterner than before.

"Frau Elheusch," he replied coldly, "the past is completely irrelevant. It really doesn't matter what happened then. We now have to look to the future of this country. We have our calling. We need to implement the orders the Führer gives us. If you don't want to follow those orders, I have to report you! It is the law, and I am here to make sure the law is being followed!"

With that, the room fell silent. Mutter, stunned, sat back down in her chair. Her mouth was slightly open. All her resistance seemed to have crumbled at this point, and she looked defeated. The room feel so quiet that the ticking of the grandfather clock coming from the hallway could be heard loud and clear.

Mutter say something! Karl urged her with his eyes.

"Alright, I'll make sure they will be at all the meetings." Mutter kept her gaze down as if she didn't want to face Albert any longer. Albert had won.

Karl could barely hide his shock.

"But, Mutter, what about all the work around here?" Hans tried to protest.

"Yes, Mutter what about the store and all the orders?" Karl chimed in.

"You heard Albert!" she hissed at both of them. "He is right. We need to support the Führer. Now you both promise Albert you will go to all the meetings!"

Karl and Hans looked at Mutter dumbfounded. Never in the past had she asked them to support the Führer. Karl was suspicious, but her stern gaze piercing through them quickly made them realize that he and Hans had better agree.

"We promise," they both obliged, nearly in unison.

A satisfied grin covered Albert's face. He had gotten what he wanted. "Good, I needed to hear that. You will not regret it. There is so much you will learn about our wonderful Führer and his plans. You will be so impressed."

Then he scanned the room, slowly, as if he suddenly remembered to look for something. "Where is his book?"

Immediately they knew he was talking about *Mein Kampf,* Hitler's manifesto. It had become the "bible" of the National Socialist German Workers' Party (Nazis).

"I have it; I can get it," Mutter responded, even more annoyed at the personal questions. *I am sure the book is not what they sent you here for!* She wanted to counter, but stayed quiet.

"Mein Kampf, of course, needs to be out in the open for anyone to see," Albert reprimanded. "You should have it sitting out here on the table, so any of your visitors can see it, and of course, so your boys can read it anytime they feel like reading Hitler's great work."

The commanding tone returned to his voice. "Go get it!"

Mutter's cheeks were even more caved in, and her narrow-set green eyes squinted. She reluctantly got up after taking in Albert's determined, matter-of-fact expression once more. Everyone in the kitchen stayed quiet while she slowly climbed up the squeaky wooden stairs to her bedroom.

She pulled open the drawer of her pressed wood, old night desk. Inside, sitting atop everything else, was the bracelet Opa had bought her at the Morgenthau's store. Underneath were a few of the books that the Nazis had handed to the kids in school or had dropped off here at their house. On the top was a children's book called *Trau keinem Fuchs auf grüner Heid und keinem Jud bei seinem Eid! (Trust No Fox on his Green Heath And No Jew on his Oath)*.

Mutter had kept all these types of books in her night desks. When they were little, she purposely had avoided reading any of them to her boys. And now that they were older, they had no interest in reading the garbage.

Hidden under the children's books, she found the red-covered *Mein Kampf* by Adolf Hitler. Quickly she grabbed it, swiped her hands over it to remove any dust, and, holding it tight, and rushed back down the steps.

"I'll keep it here," she announced, and placed the book in the middle of the kitchen table in an attempt to appease Albert.

"It looks brand-new!" Albert picked it up and flipped through it, his black eyebrows rolled up in surprise.

"I am taking good care of it!" Mutter defended.

"Alright, well then, make sure your boys read it. They will be quizzed about it at the Hitler Youth!" Albert ordered again. Mutter just nodded silently.

Now content, Albert turned back to the family. "Come on now! Let's do the Hitler salute."

He angled his arm at forty-five degrees, bellowed "Heil Hitler!" and encouraged the boys to copy him. Karl and Hans reluctantly, and almost embarrassed, followed suit. Clicking his heels, right hand extended, Albert left them with a second loud, "Heil Hitler!" He marched out the door stepping high and full of pride.

As soon as Albert slammed the door behind him, Karl ran up to it, turned the heavy iron key, and locked it.

"We need to remember to keep this door locked!" He exhaled, then turned around. "Mutter?" he asked, studying her face.

"Sssshhhhhh!"

Mutter put a finger to her lips and lowered her voice. "Have you heard about Mr. Morgenthau?" she whispered. Karl wasn't too surprised that Mutter already knew. Before he could respond she continued.

"Mr. Morgenthau was taken in for questioning." She shook her head. "It is a bad sign that he was here. Albert is not to be trusted. His entire family is not to be trusted. His father led the arrest, and they are one of the many enforcing these laws. We need to just do exactly what he says. I don't want any of us to be arrested and end up in a camp; we need to stick together. Just go along with it for now."

Then she whispered even lower, "We don't have to do it for much longer. The Allied soldiers are coming. I heard it on the radio. Hitler doesn't have much time left."

"Mutter, you know you are not allowed to listen to those radio stations," Hans scolded. "What if we get caught? We will all get arrested!"

Karl, also worried, chimed in in support. "Mutter, yes, please stop listening to those stations!"

"I am careful about the stations. You know I only play them at the lowest volume. And lately, I have been putting a sheet over my head when I listen." She chuckled at herself for a split second, and then quickly became serious again. "You have to be more careful about yourselves! Go to those meetings, agree to what they say. Just pretend you agree. It's not for much longer."

The boys wanted to explain to her that her radio signals could be traced, but the conversation was over.

"Hurry and eat—we still have work to do!" Mutter ordered.

Karl would have to wait another night to ask "the question." He had asked Daniel to come back that night, anticipating having an answer for him. But now he would just have to tell him that he needed to wait another day.

Chapter 4:

The Furniture Order

September 30, 1944

It was late afternoon. Using the old broom, Karl feverishly swept wood chips and sawdust off the worn carpentry floor. The broom's bristles were so sparse it took Karl several repeated strokes to get the chips into a pile.

It was nearing the end of another long workday, and Opa was sitting down at the other end of the room sanding an unfinished chair that he was restoring for one of the neighbors. Now in his seventies, Opa's legs were too weak to allow him to stand for too long, and it was too difficult for him to bend down. So sitting with the chair in his lap seemed to be the most practical way of getting the sanding done.

Suddenly, and without a knock, the downstairs store door ripped open. The rusty bell hanging off it on a worn-out string rattled louder than usual against the wooden frame, as if to complain about the unexpected interruption.

An SS soldier appeared in the door frame. He was in his late thirties, with sculpted features, high cheekbones, and black hair that was cut short. He was around the same height as Karl, who now at sixteen was five-foot-eight. The soldier's dark piercing eyes glared at them. Startled, Opa and Karl stopped mid-work and stared back at the unexpected intruder.

Recognizing the officer as one of the SS, Opa gasped nervously, noticed only by Karl, and leaned back into the shadow of the room where the window's late afternoon sunlight didn't reach. Karl dropped his broom, immediately jumped to attention, and saluted.

"Heil Hitler!"

The salute was mutual, Karl's and the soldier's heels clicking in time. The Hitler Youth training, which he and Hans had been attending diligently since Albert threatened them in their kitchen over a year ago, had taught him this required response: the right arm had to be slanted and stretched out at eye level, with the hand flat and facing down. Not using the extended arm signal and the customary greeting would have been considered a grave disrespect, chargeable with immediate arrest.

"May I help you, Herr Major?" asked Karl, only lowering his right arm from the salute after the officer did so. Karl had long ago learned to read the ranks by the uniform insignia, and quickly identified this soldier's rank.

"Major Hildenberg." He introduced himself in a deep, raspy voice. "I need an oak desk!" he demanded without any further introduction. The Major took off his black leather gloves and tapped his right hand's fingertips with them as he spoke. His appearance, with his shiny boots and pressed uniform, was impeccable. Karl and Opa stared at him in anticipation as the Major continued.

"I need you to build me an oak desk and a matching oak chair. It needs to meet specific requirements. It is for a special visitor to the town. He is expected here Friday, in one week! We need a day to transport it and set it up in our office, so…," he hesitated to allow himself time to add the days. "Can you have it all done by next Wednesday?"

One week isn't nearly enough time for building an oak desk! Karl reacted in panic. But glancing at his Opa and seeing him nod energetically, Karl answered quickly, "Yes, Sir. Of course, Herr Major! Can we hear the specs? What design do you have in mind?"

"Sketch it as I describe it!" the Major ordered. "I want to make sure we have a mutual agreement. There is no room for misunderstanding."

Opa shuffled as fast as he could toward the desk near the wall and frantically opened the old wooden drawers, not daring to turn his back to the SS officer as he pulled out a Faber pencil. The Major sensed Opa's uneasiness and kept his dark brown, mistrusting eyes focused on Opa's every move.

With his arthritis-stricken and bent hands, Opa handed the pencil and paper to Karl, who then cautiously motioned to the Major to have a seat at the wooden table that was planted in the middle of the small carpentry. Karl also rushed over to it, and with his sleeves, quickly wiped off a few specks of sawdust.

"Opa, I will need a ruler." Karl nodded at the old wooden ruler visible in the drawer. Opa quickly obliged and handed it to Karl.

Major Hildenberg took off his light-grey military cap and placed it at the end of the table, and then dragged the old chair up to the table. He sat down with one of his legs extended to the side, appearing to be ready to jump up at a moment's notice.

Karl sat down on the opposite side of the Major, glancing down at the piece of paper, gesturing with the pencil to show his eagerness to start drawing. "I am ready, Herr Major," he said.

"The oak desk's front edge should be the shape of a wave." The Major's large tan hand made a long horizontal up-and-down wave motion. "The front of the desk needs to be two meters wide, and the sides one meter deep."

Karl's eyes widened ever so slightly as he tried to imagine the unusually shaped desk, but he remained quiet and tried hard to keep his facial expressions neutral. He worked fiercely with his pencil to recreate the Major's thoughts on paper, sketching it as best as he could, while the Major demanded he measure and draw the desk to size.

"Draw it to a ten centimeter to one meter ratio," he demanded. "Also, I want the desk to be black. Black lacquer. It needs to shine!"

Karl continued to wonder, *Black? Why would anyone paint an oak desk black? It will look like a piano. Why not leave the natural color of the oak and at most seal it?* Karl did not dare to question the Major, however, and continued to draw the desk model to meet the design. The Major watched Karl's every mark as he used the old ruler to draw the unusually-shaped desk, requiring him to modify the shapes here and there.

The soldier also continued to describe his demands: "The legs should have the same shape as the front of the desk—the shape of a wave." *That surely will make things difficult!* Karl thought but remained quiet.

"The legs shall give enough room so anyone a bit heavier can comfortably push the chair under the desk and sit in it. Of course, the chair color is to match the desk, so paint it black also," the Major continued. "The back of the chairs also needs to be wave-shaped to match the desk's design."

"Of course," muttered Karl, his disagreement starting to show ever so slightly.

The Major caught into the shift immediately. "Of course, what?" he demanded, eyes squinted at Karl.

"Of course, Herr Major. I am in agreement with you, and, of course, the table will be the same color as the desk," Karl responded, softly appeasing the Major while keeping his head down.

After much erasing, clarifying and modifying the unusual custom desk and chair design, Karl finally came up with a draft with which the Major finally seemed satisfied.

Then the Major's eyebrows rose. "When are you starting on this?" he inquired. "I want to see progress as it's being built. I need to make sure it is exactly as we want it."

With his black gloves, the Major pointed and tapped to the rough sketch of the furniture outline on the piece of paper. Karl was still feverishly adding finishing touches, smoothing out edges, blowing away the eraser slivers and adding final lines.

Before Karl could look up to answer, the Major repeated his demand, agitated. "This date cannot be missed!"

Karl jumped up, saluting. "If you permit me, Herr Major, I am very sure we have the wood, but let me check the storage area in the back to be one-hundred percent sure we have the specific size of oak wood needed for this order."

Without waiting for approval, Karl grabbed the drawing and headed for the shed.

"Well, you'd better, or—" Before the Major could finish, Karl had already opened the door to the adjacent wood storage.

The Major mumbled to himself, but Opa couldn't make out what he said. He instead chose to put the chair back on his lap and continue sanding it.

Karl had one large piece of oak in mind, but before fully committing to that important deadline, he needed to measure the size of it to make sure they could accommodate the unusual order.

The heavy door to the dimly lit storage room squeaked eerily as Karl opened it. *I need some drops to oil this door*, Karl thought as he had so many times before. It was all so much easier when Uncle Joseph was still with them. Because Karl had lost his father so early, his uncle had been a father figure to him, and at times like these, he missed him more than ever.

The penetrating smell of wood immediately surrounded him. Karl looked through the stacks of oak. The wood was neatly lined up, stacked by size and organized by type, and the familiar aroma of wood resin hovered in the air. He liked the smell. It was something he grew up with.

Using Opa's old tractor, they had pulled the trunks from the forest on the ten acres of land that Opa owned. Using their saw, Karl and his brother Hans had cut the huge tree trunks into nice-sized sheets in Opa's backyard before moving them in here. This was hard labor and a lot of work, but Karl had never minded it. Sometimes Daniel would help out as well, making the chores more bearable and fun. Daniel was not only a hard worker, but he also had a great sense of humor, lightening the mood with his jokes and shenanigans.

Daniel!

Karl thought of his friend often. He had not seen him since the night he had asked Karl if his family could hide them. Karl had told him to come back, and then Albert had intruded upon their dinner, thwarting Karl's plans to ask Mutter and Opa.

Daniel never showed up that night, and Karl had wondered whether Daniel perhaps had stumbled upon Albert leaving the house and ducked away. Or maybe Karl had slept so deeply he had never heard Daniel's pebbles against the window.

Karl had waited a couple of nights for Daniel to reappear; when he didn't, Karl grew worried. He still had not asked Mutter and Opa the question, but, five days later, during early dusk, he bundled up and rode his bike to Daniel's home to check on him.

The roads had been cleared of the snow that had fallen the night Daniel had visited. The cobblestones were slick, and Karl repeatedly slipped; but he was determined to check on Daniel and his little family.

When he got to Daniel's home, he found it vacant. The store's upstairs was dark. No smoke rose from the chimney as it did from the neighboring houses. The snow covering the steps leading upstairs had been untouched, sparkling in the moonlight.

Karl stared in disbelief. The only small jewelry store in their entire village had been boarded up and shut down by the Nazis. Karl remembered how Mutter had always wished she could afford anything in that store—the jewelry was beautiful, and she loved going there just to look and dream about having that one specific white pearl bracelet. Then, on the 10th anniversary of Karl's father's death, Opa had surprised Mutter with that very bracelet as a gift.

At first, Mutter scolded Opa for splurging so much, when they had so little. But then she learned that Opa he had built a chest of drawers for the Morgenthaus in return. The Morgenthau's were really good people.

Karl remembered how upset Opa and Mutter were when the store was shuttered down, and the "closed" sign was hung and the huge Star of David was painted on the front. The Morgenthaus had continued living upstairs, then.

And even though it was obvious that nobody would be there that night, Karl got off his bike, climbed up the curving stone steps, leaving the first foot prints in the untouched snow, and knocked on the upstairs entrance door.

There was no answer.

Karl waited a few minutes, but was met with only painful silence. Guilt and worry rose in his chest as he finally got back on his bike and left. What if they could have possibly helped Daniel, and his Mom and sister, but failed?

That night, Karl had gone home to tell Mutter about his fear for the Morgenthau family. He also told her that Daniel and his mom had asked him about hiding them, but that he didn't think she would have approved, and that they were no longer living at the old store, and—

In his panic and grief, the words were all rushing out. But Mutter grabbed his hand and told him to calm down. She confided in him that she had heard from the baker's wife just the other day that Daniel and his family had moved in with the grandparents on the mother's side, ten kilometers down the road in the nearby Nuernberg outskirts.

"But," Mutter whispered, "nobody is allowed to know."

Karl was so relieved at the time, he almost wanted to cry. Of course Karl wouldn't tell anyone—not even his brothers. He was just glad that the family had found a seemingly safe place to stay.

Now that he knew where they were, Karl committed to visiting Daniel sometime soon, despite everyone telling him to stay away from "that Jew." During the Hitler Youth meetings, they were told over and over again to stay away from non-Arian blood. Karl rolled his eyes just at the thought of those teachings. He had always wanted to visit his friend soon regardless of the propaganda, ride his bike the distance to the outskirts.

But now here he was, over three years later, and he still had not seen or heard from Daniel. He had been so busy working on supporting his Opa's store, Mutter and brothers, helping with the carpentry work, attending Hitler Youth meetings and all the holiday marches.

Hitler had invented more holidays for various reasons, such as the "Heroes' Memorial Day" on March 16th, Hitler's birthday on April

20th, Labor Day on May 1st, and others. Each required much preparation and was overly time-consuming to attend. Karl would have preferred to avoid all of the Nazi fanfare, but as a Hitler Youth, he had been forced to participate.

Karl had been standing there in deep thought. The Major was waiting on him! He quickly glanced back over the stacks of wood.

Their supply was starting to run low. There was not much stored wood left until summer, and when Karl finally found the perfect oak pieces in front of him, he was relieved.

These pieces were from the oak tree that had taken Hans, Daniel, Opa, and even Mutter, days to chop up and store away. It was an old oak tree saved for a special occasion. Karl had dreamed of showing off his carpentry skills to the world using these huge chunks of oak someday. "Now," he sighed, "it will be used for this Major's furniture order."

But Karl recognized this was an incredibly important order, important to Opa, his family, and to their very livelihood. The Munich events and the Morgenthau's disappearance were just two of the many examples that had everyone scared to death.

Taking out his meter stick, he measured the beautiful oak's length and width. He touched it to feel and verify its quality, and roughly measured it again to double-check, even though experience and his keen eye knew the size would be adequate for the Major's order. Then Karl held up the drawing to study it again, imagining how he would shape the wood chunks into the requested design. It would take thick boards to make the table top, he noted.

Closing the wooden door to the shed, Karl returned to the front room where Opa and the Major were both pretending the other was not present. They looked as though they had not spoken a word.

The relief apparent on his face, Karl turned to the Major. "*Jawohl*, Herr Major. We can have the order ready in time," he beamed, and quickly glanced confidently over at Opa, who was watching everything unfold from the back of the room. Though he seemed determined to stay uninvolved, Karl noticed his slight exhale as he leaned forward.

The Major's lips formed a quick smile, so fleeting that Karl later doubted whether it had ever been there.

Major Hildenberg officially signed the sketch Karl handed to him, scribbled the due date and made Karl sign it. This paper was to be considered a contract, and the Major repeated that he would be back in the next couple days to witness progress. He added, in a low but undoubtedly threatening tone, leaning in toward Karl, as if Opa was not supposed to hear the intimidation, looking firmly into Karl's eyes: "I expect *quality* furniture. If you deliver in time, and to my satisfaction, I will reward you. If the order is not ready in time, there will be consequences."

Quickly saluting, the Major turned a sharp 180-degrees and strutted out. Karl made an attempt to return the salute, but the Major had turned around so quickly that Karl dropped his hand mid-salute—it was unimportant once the Major had left.

Karl stood, almost paralyzed, staring at the door, the tiny bell above it still vibrating. With the threatening words still hanging in the air,

Karl and Opa both were imagining the types of consequences the Major was referring to.

Suddenly, Opa frantically broke the silence. "Karl, let's get started on this now! I know it's late, but can you get Hans, so you two can drag the oak in here, and we can get started?" Karl could already feel Opa's anxiety.

"*Ja!*" Karl quickly ran upstairs past Mutter, who was in the kitchen, wearing her grey apron and cutting potatoes to prepare a soup with the few ingredients she could find. "Where is Hans, Mutter?" he asked hastily, scanning the kitchen for his brother.

"He's in his room," she responded, looking up from cutting. She could sense the worry in Karl's voice. "What's wrong?"

But Karl was already darting upstairs to find Hans. His brother was lying in bed reading the Bible, underlining noteworthy verses as he did so often, completely oblivious to his surroundings.

"Hans, put that away! You need to hide it! An SS Major was just here!"

Hans quickly covered the Bible under his blanket.

"He left," Karl continued. "He ordered an oak desk. He wants it wave-shaped, and black lacquered with a matching chair. And it all has to be ready to be delivered by Wednesday of next week!"

Hans' eyes widened. "Wait. Slow down... That's impossible!"

"Opa and I both will have to work around the clock. We'll just need to get it done. You need to help, too. We want to get started right away."

Grasping the urgency, Hans immediately jumped out of bed, slid into his slippers, and followed Karl downstairs. They heard Mutter calling, "Soup's ready in a minute!" as they passed by the kitchen.

"Mutter, please bring it downstairs," Hans quickly responded. "We don't have time to sit down and eat."

Determined to deliver the furniture order in time, Karl snatched the sketch off the table where he had left it, and with it, they marched into the back room.

"You grab this end and I'll grab this one," he said to Hans, pointing at the oak as he handed the sketch to Opa, who had followed to oversee it all.

Meticulously measuring and sawing the pieces as sweat dripped into their eyes, holding the pieces and sizing them up against each other, Karl and Opa began to build the unusually shaped oak desk. Karl didn't hammer, but rather carefully chiseled the nails into the wood. He wanted the desk and chair to be of especially high quality. Their very lives depended on it.

Mutter came downstairs with three bowls of steaming soup balanced on a tray and set them down carefully at the desk by the wall. "Here you go!" she announced before heading back upstairs.

Opa and the boys worked ceaselessly until the early morning hours when finally, completely exhausted, they went to sleep.

****

October 5, 1944

Karl dreaded and despised each Hitler Youth meeting. Especially this particular week, when he much preferred to be in Opa's little carpentry working on the Major's desk. But he had no choice but to attend each of the required gatherings.

Sitting in half circles in their meeting hall, the youth heard that day from Albert—who was leading Karl's group—about the *Spitzel* (spies) who turned in anyone who uttered even the slightest negative word about Hitler. Albert told the story of two students who had written up their teacher preaching against the regime. He now needed one of the Hitler Youth boys to sit in one of this teacher's classes to catch him fresh-handed. Albert was trying to recruit *Spitzels*, but Karl didn't want to be part of it.

"Karl, you haven't been to school in a while. He wouldn't suspect you!" Albert exclaimed, his eyes taunting Karl to sign up for the spy work.

But Karl shook his head. "No, I have a furniture order from a Major that I need to work on. We have a tight deadline for it, next Wednesday," he replied. And to his relief, Albert quickly accepted. Everyone knew a Major's order was to be taken very seriously.

That moment, Karl was actually thankful to the Major for placing this order, because it gave him an acceptable excuse. Karl would do anything to avoid becoming like the janitor who ratted out the Scholz siblings for dropping leaflets, and who was ultimately responsible for their execution.

How could this janitor live with himself? Those young students with a bright future beheaded only because they stood up for their beliefs!

The tragic story of the Scholz brother and sister was one of many that would continue to haunt Karl.

Who would the poor boy be that would be selected to spy on this teacher to turn him in? Karl wished he could warn that teacher, but there were so many spies everywhere—even getting near him would be too risky.

After Albert's address, the meeting moved outdoors, and it was time for marching practice. They were ordered to line up and march to the nearest forest, Albert leading them along.

On this particular day, they were going to apply their newly-learned skills on how to use a compass.

They marched through the cobblestone village streets. A sea of red flags and the swastika stickers hung from almost everyone's house.

The muffled sounds of marching steps and chanting grew increasingly louder, the droning sound disrupting the calm of this beautiful fall display as they got closer to the countryside of Southern Germany.

A group of robins who hadn't started their migration yet sipped the water from the small creek that had formed from an earlier rain shower. As the troops got closer, the birds scurried. Yet Karl still felt relieved to be simply out in nature, away from all the Nazi symbolism, and away from the swastika flags and Nazi signs everywhere.

It was October of 1944, five years into World War II. Karl was taller now, and more muscular. He marched as part of his Troop B, stepping the goose-step along with his teenage friends, swiftly kicking their stiff legs up and down in unison like synchronized robots. They marched with their right arms extended stiffly to form the 'Heil Hitler' salute, guns holstered over their left shoulders, heads turned. Karl, with his red curls and hazel eyes, wore a chiseled facial expression that was cold and distant for such a young man. His movements were mechanical, his mind absent from the present. He had become skilled in marching along, involuntarily, without any inner conviction, and joining in their chants:

I once had a comrade
You will not find a better one
The drum called to battle
He walked at my side
In the same pace and step
A bullet came flying
Is it my turn or yours?
He was ripped away
He lies at my feet
As if it was a part of me

As Karl's lips moved to the rhetoric of the chants his thoughts drifted to his frail Opa, to Mutter, and to their carpentry. More than ever that day, Karl resented the drill, regimentation, political indoctrination, enforced uniformity, and lack of freedom and suppression of individual expression that the Hitler Youth membership imposed on him. Just when most kids wanted to experiment and become their own persons, the Hitler Youth demanded conformity to traditional values, limiting any growth. Smoking, drinking, partying and sex were criminalized eventually, and the Nazis depended on Hitler Youth patrols to enforce the strict restrictions it placed on youthful behavior.

According to the Law for the Protection of Youth of March 9, 1940, young people under eighteen were banned from the streets after dark and could not frequent bars, restaurants, cinemas, or other places of entertainment after nine o'clock in the evening if unaccompanied by an adult. It was made illegal for youths under sixteen to smoke in public or to be served spirits.[iv]

Karl was not interested in getting drunk or smoking, but he still despised the numerous restrictions.

It was clear to him that the Nazis didn't have any good intentions for Germany. And what really baffled Karl was that Hitler wasn't even German-born, but had been born in Austria.

Marching and chanting along the German countryside, all Karl could imagine was the half-finished oak desk and chair, just as he had sketched it, and all the work that still had to get done.

".....a bullet came flying" they repeated the chants as they continued to goose-step.

Who might that important visitor be the Major had referred to? Could it be that he was referring to the Führer himself?

It could be easily possible that Hitler was coming. The Führer's headquarters were only twenty-four kilometers down the road from Karl's home, and it seemed that it had to be a very important visitor for the Major to feel this strongly about this exact date. But Karl had also heard that Hitler was hiding out in the Eagles Nest in Berchtesgaden, and the Major had mentioned a heavy-set person.

Who could it be?

The Major promised that Karl would be well compensated, if the desk was delivered in time. This furniture order would mean additional food on the table for Karl's family. They had no other option, but to deliver.

"Mein Vaterland, über alles..." he heard himself say. "My Fatherland, above all of them...." Karl didn't believe in any of the words his lips were forming during these absurd chants. Above all of the countries? Why were they trying to instill the idea in citizens that Germany was superior to the rest of the world? What had happened to the country he had grown up in, the country he knew? So much had changed since the war began five years ago.

When the youth finally arrived at the forest, they were divided into two teams: one would have to hide in the nearby woods, and the other was tasked with searching for them. Karl despised these games, though he knew they were to gain important skills for defending themselves in a war. These survival skills were necessary at this point of the war, with Germany retreating at all fronts and with many of the enemy soldiers already fighting in the German forests.

That day, Karl used his compass to purposely hide deep in the forest where he could relax, and try to enjoy the calm of nature as he sat behind a tree on the soft moss. He would not return until he was sure it was time for the entire group to march back. When he did finally step out of the forest, having successfully used his compass to find his way back, he re-joined his group. Albert gave him an all-knowing look, but for some reason decided not to belabor him. Karl looked away. Maybe Albert gave Karl a break because he must have known the pressure Karl was under to get this furniture order completed in time.

The group marched back, and at long last, they were dismissed from the mandatory Saturday Hitler Youth drills. Karl raced home in his heavy, black Hitler Youth boots. Once inside, he hollered into the kitchen, "Mutter, can you bring the soup downstairs again? I have to continue working on the 'Major desk'," as it came to be called, and he quickly disappeared into the carpentry shop.

Chapter 5
SS

After having feverishly worked on the "Major desk" for several days, Karl started to feel confident that the order would be ready by the Wednesday deadline. The Major was scheduled to personally check again on the progress the next day, and Karl expected that he would be happy with the progress so far. The piece of oak already had the beautiful majestic wave shape, exactly the dimensions the Major had asked for, and it was turning out to look more exquisite than Karl could have imagined.

It was close to midnight; although exhausted, Karl was lying in bed wide awake. He should have been asleep, between the Hitler Youth gatherings and the marching outside all day, then the continued sanding, hammering and chiseling of the desk. But all the stories floating in his mind were keeping him awake.

His worried thoughts drifted again to the Scholl siblings, the young students who spoke up against Hitler and were executed over a year ago. They were only kids, only a year or two older than Karl's oldest brother, Hermann. Karl also worried about the teacher whom some of his comrades in the Hitler Youth had turned in. What would happen to him?

He thought of the others who tried to speak up or had gone as far as to try to assassinate Hitler, such as Claus Schenk Graf von Stauffenberg. Claus, together with others, had attempted to kill Hitler this past July. He had hoped that, with Hitler dead, they could remove the Nazi Party from power. How did the attempt fail? Karl lay there imagining how it all went wrong. He had heard bits and pieces from others in the Hitler Youth. Unfortunately, Hitler was only barely injured in this assassination attempt. How did Hitler continue to escape these attacks?

Stauffenberg was expeditiously executed by firing squad. Karl didn't know how they had traced the attack back to Stauffenberg, but it was clear there were enough Spitzels everywhere, and nobody could be trusted.

He wished he were older so he could help more, but he was just sixteen years old then, without any power. If he was older, he would support any freedom fighters. He imagined how he would succeed in helping with the assassination. Somebody needed to finally stop Hitler.

Karl lay there tossing and turning, wondering what it would mean for Germany and to his family if this war were finally over, or if the assassination attempts would have been successful. Or better yet, what if Hitler had been accepted by that art school he applied to multiple times? Or if Hitler had been killed during his service in World War I? There were so many "ifs", Karl could only dream of.

He despised Hitler for many reasons. If it weren't for Hitler and his regime, Karl would now be finishing his carpentry apprenticeship at the renowned *Nürnberg Schreinerei* (carpentry). Although Opa was very skilled in teaching him the basics, Karl wanted to gain the newest woodcarving skills that Opa could not teach him. Karl sighed at the lost opportunity, and then his thoughts drifted on to his Jewish friend, Daniel Morgenthau.

He had lost all contact with Daniel. Still nobody knew where the family had been taken. Karl hoped he would hear from them soon.

He then thought about his Uncle Joseph, another close person missing from his life. *Where was he?* It still bothered Karl that they had not heard from him either. He must be dead; Karl was convinced.

One worried thought led to another. Karl sighed deeply and started to think of all the work ahead of him the next day. Not only did he need to work on the Major's desk, but he had yet another Hitler Youth meeting first thing in the morning. He really needed to get some sleep…

Suddenly, there was a loud knock on their front door. Sleep was destined never to come.

That was the cold, rainy October night the SS Albert and Ferdinand ripped him and his two brothers out of their home against their will. He recalled Mutter crying, trying to be strong while waving goodbye as they all were marched out the door. He still remembered her final pleading words to them: "Stay together! Look out for each other!" Then she broke down sobbing, covering her wrinkled face with her weathered hands. Mutter was dealing with the nearly unbearable pain of losing her three sons in one night.

"Goodbye, Mutter!" Hans and Karl had both responded, one last time, while Ferdinand rolled Hermann out, who just lifted his hand up for a slight wave goodbye. And as fast as they had come that night, the SS soldiers slammed the big oak front door shut behind them. The house fell silent.

Hans tried to look back as they walked down the alley toward the idling SS truck, but Albert ordered them, "Straight ahead, boys! Straight ahead!" They had no other choice but to march toward the marked *Kübelwagen* parked outside awaiting them.

The cold rain pounded the lifeless cobblestone as Albert directed the boys to get into the back seat, pushing each of their heads down. They quickly climbed in, Hans sliding over to make room for Karl.

They looked out the wet window, camouflaged in raindrops, and watched Ferdinand lift Hermann from his wheelchair into the back of his *Kübelcar* parked in front of them. Hermann was very skinny—he needed to remain that way to be able to easily get around in his wheelchair—but Ferdinand's knees still nearly buckled under his weight. The emotional pain Karl and Hans felt was nearly unbearable, as they helplessly had to look on as their handicapped brother vanished into the car in front of them.

Albert started the wagon, pulled out, and drove past Ferdinand's car. Both Hans and Karl turned their heads, trying to get one last glimpse of their brother. But it was too dark and rainy. All they could see was the rain-covered window. They reluctantly turned around and, overwhelmed, slumped back into the back seat of the wagon.

"Where are you taking us, Albert?" Hans dared to ask as he stared straight ahead.

"To the SS Headquarters," Albert snapped. "And for the last time, to both of you I am SS-Scharführer Albert Wüst! Don't call me by my first name ever again! That's an order!"

He got promoted. That was fast! Karl and Hans glanced at each other. They knew how to read ranks, and could easily imagine why Albert had moved up so quickly: leading all the *Spitzels* in the Hitler Youth was surely one of the qualities that helped him get there.

Karl knew where the SS Headquarters was located. He had walked by grey stone, majestic 18th century building with its large "SS *Hauptquartier*" sign on the front many times, and he had seen the many SS soldiers coming and going from there constantly.

The ride over cobblestones, only a few miles down the road toward the western outskirts of Nürnberg, was quiet. In the back seat, Hans and Karl, leaned back, both with their arms crossed in front of them, exchanging glances every now and then.

Only ten minutes had passed when Albert slowed to a stop, parking the wagon on the side of the grey brick buildings—the SS barracks.

"Get out. We are heading to the central main SS building there," Albert ordered the two brothers, pointing toward the majestic building at the center of the SS barracks. It had two side wings, both surrounding a courtyard.

Inside, soldiers and civilians were rushing around as if everyone was in a big hurry to get someplace, even though it was the middle of the night.

Albert handed over Hans and Karl to the first soldier he came across as they walked in.

"These are the Elheusch boys I mentioned; they are all yours. Get them registered." Albert saluted, clicked his heels, and walked away in the opposite direction, not saying another word to either brother.

Karl couldn't believe this was the same Albert they had played with in the backyard just a few years ago. It couldn't be real that Albert, their former neighborhood friend, had just delivered them to the SS. They were living their worst nightmare. And Herman in a home? Karl couldn't stop worrying about that. What did that mean? What home?

"Follow me," the short, chubby SS-*Rottenführer* with a name tag reading "Schmidt" ordered the boys as he started waddling down a long hallway, expecting them to follow. He stopped and pushed down the cast metal door handle to the first door, which lead to a large room where a big-bellied SS corporal was sitting at a small desk right at the entrance.

"Sign in here," demanded the overweight corporal with a name tag "Bäcker". He handed each of them forms to fill out.

Karl and Hans wrote in the information requested on the form: Name, Address, Age, Birthdate, member of Hitler Youth Y/N, Father in the Army Y/N, Profession, and so on.

"Leave the blood type field empty. That's what we'll figure out here."

The boys handed the filled-out forms back to Bäcker.

"Now, find an empty station," he said as he pointed into the general room area.

Hans and Karl stepped into the room and looked around at the large area, which was laid out to serve as a makeshift hospital room. There were tables and chairs set up with women in nursing gear, drawing blood from numerous boys dressed in Hitler Youth uniforms.

"Sit down and get your blood drawn," one of the SS soldiers commanded Hans and Karl as he pointed toward a few empty stations. They must have gathered all the boys from the neighborhood. Karl saw some familiar faces that looked up at him tiredly to give him a slight nod. He recognized Martin from his Hitler Youth group, who barely acknowledged Karl, probably too upset about his fate.

Hans and Karl looked at each other, and then Hans asked the SS, "Why do they need to take our blood?"

"Just get it done and don't ask!" was his impatient response.

"They need to know your blood type in case you need a blood transfusion," Karl whispered to Hans.

It was finally sinking in—they were going to war. Karl had heard on Mutter's radio that Hitler was pulling in the young and the old: men and women under sixty and boys and girls as young as twelve. With the Allied forces advancing, Hitler was desperate. So many lives had already been lost in this war, hundreds of thousands of casualties. There was hardly anyone left to fight, and this was Hitler's last attempt at winning it. Hans had also heard on Mutter's radio that the Allied forces had already invaded Italy, one of Germany's few allies, and they had also already liberated France. Germany was retreating on all fronts.

"Make a fist," said the boyish nurse wearing brown, thick-rimmed glasses, her eyes barely noticeable. She flashed a crooked toothed smile as she unbuttoned Karl's shirt sleeve, rolling it back for him before he could get to it.

She tied a rubber band around his upper arm.

"You have nice veins. It's easy to get blood with these perfect veins," she said as she tapped on his right arm. Her words drew a slight smile from Karl. Then, without another warning, she stuck his arm with the needle.

"Yuk!" he said as he watched his blood seep into the tube. Karl had never been too fond of blood.

Then before he knew it, the nurse was done.

"Sit here and wait for the results," she ordered him, and then repeated the same procedure for Hans.

By the time they had finished having their blood drawn, the large rectangular clock hanging from the center wall of the room showed 2 a.m. Exhaustion was beginning to set in. Even the hard wooden benches looked inviting to sleep on, and nobody objected when they laid down and quickly fell asleep.

It seemed like Karl had just drifted off when the nurse was shaking him awake again. The morning's first daylight was streaming through the wide gothic windows into the makeshift hospital room, where hundreds of boys were strewn throughout, sleeping on the floors and benches.

"Here are your results," she said in a soft and tired voice. She must have been working all night. With a light touch of her hand on his shoulder, she handed him a piece of paper.

Karl was told he was just type "A", while Hans was type "A and ready for the tropics". Karl had heard, whether true or not, that Rommel took only type "A" soldiers to the desert in Africa because it was easier to exchange blood that way, but it had to be type "A ready for tropics." While the Rhesus factor had been discovered in 1937, it was not being used yet to distinguish blood types.

Karl immediately remarked, "Hans, hopefully you don't have to go to Africa while I have to stay here. I want us to stay together."

"I think the war in Africa is lost," Hans replied, but before Karl could respond, the nurse came back.

"Now we'll need to tattoo your blood type into your underarm near the armpit," she told them.

"A tattoo?" Both boys' mouths dropped open.

They noticed then that the other boys were getting ready to be tattooed. They had no choice. As the medic tattooed their underarms, most boys remained stoic, gritting their teeth. They didn't want to show weakness, even though it was one of the most painful areas to get a tattoo. The hypothermic needle stabbed over and over until the "A" was burned into their skin. After the tattoo, Karl couldn't lift his arm for three days.

"Arghhhhhhhh!"

A few of the boys screamed out loud. Karl recognized one from his school before he had dropped out to help more with the carpentry.

The boy's name was Alois. He always had been one of the more studious kids in class. *All that hard work apparently hasn't paid off,* Karl thought grimly. *And he now is also here being prepared for war, just like the rest of us.*

Once they were tattooed, the corporal ordered them to line up in the largest hall located in the center of the compound, out the door to the right and straight down the hallway. They followed the directions, unsure of what awaited them.

Chapter 6
War

Once tattooed, all three hundred boys were handed nicely-pressed, field-gray SS uniforms, black leather belts, SS jackets, and black, shiny boots. They were ordered to change into the new attire right there. Karl and Hans could barely move their arms; their freshly tattooed underarms made it painful and slow to change into their shirts. A lot of moaning and groaning could be heard from the other boys as well.

Once dressed, they were all ordered to pile their old clothes into a corner, from where they would later be collected. Then they stood around, huddled in the largest hall of the central main building in the cold SS compound, waiting. *What would their next orders be? Where would they be fighting?*

Some were whispering thin speculations, but nobody wanted to draw attention. They knew that the Russians and Americans were advancing on both the Eastern and Western fronts, with massive air bombardments and ground movements against the German soldiers. A few were whispering about the latest news they had heard, and they debated how much of a difference, if any, they could make at this point. Wasn't it too late to do anything? They were all anxiously awaiting their fate.

The large double doors at the end of the hall swung open, and all heads turned in that direction. A sergeant with the name "Mauer" meticulously embroidered on his uniform stepped through the doorway, flanked on each side by a captain.

The *Hauptmann*, without looking left or right, marched straight toward the hall's prominent podium located at the front center stage. The morning sunbeams were streaming through the large stained-glass windows directly onto the podium, as if a spotlight was shining on the new arrival. The two captains followed the Hauptmann in cadence. The trio's sudden and seemingly rehearsed appearance underlined that something very important was about to take place. The boys' steady mumbling immediately ceased and an anticipatory silence blanketed the room. All eyes were directed at the Hauptmann standing at the podium.

Hauptmann Mauer was a middle-aged, stocky man with fat red checks, blotchy skin, and small, dark, narrow-set eyes. Judging by his sizable belly and the enlarged capillaries on his oversized nose, drinking beer and Schnapps might have been one of his favorite pastimes. *Drinking is one way to cope,* Karl thought.

The Hauptmann's bloated head barely appeared a few inches above the podium, his body nearly swallowed whole behind it. The two young captains standing by his sides towered over him.

"Heil Hitler!" Hauptmann Mauer shouted at the top of his lungs, sounding very angry. Then he sternly saluted with the common arm gesture, heels clicking, his fat arm stretched out above the lectern. "Heil Hitler!" the boys immediately responded back in chorus, returning the salute.

"Welcome! You are here because we are counting on you! *Hitler* is counting on you! You are needed to help build the Thousand-year

Reich! It is an honor to be part of this endeavor! I am proud to be part of it!"

He paused.

"Now, repeat after me!" Mauer ordered the boys, in a loud, commanding voice. "'I swear to fight and defend my Vaterland until my death!'"

The boys attempted to repeat the sentence; some spoke the words faster, while others just mumbled: "I swear... I swear... to fight ... fight ... and defend my Vaterland until my death." The response was woefully out of sync.

Mauer's hands immediately grasped his hips and impatiently he screamed, "Show me you mean it! Show me you are in for the fight of the Thousand-year Reich until your death! Tell me you will fight for the Thousand-year Reich! Louder! And uniformly this time! Especially you there!" He pointed his fat finger at one of the pimple-faced young recruits in the front row with the nametag "Bach". "Do your lips move?"

Realizing he was Mauer's target, the young, red-faced soldier quickly responded with a firm "Yes, sir!" with a salute and heels clicking.

" 'Yes, sir' what!" Mauer demanded, his eyes piercing into the helpless boy.

"Yes, sir, I will fight for my Vaterland until my death! I will fight for the Thousand-year Reich!" the recruit responded firmly, emphasizing each word.

Karl pitied the fresh-faced boy, but at the same time was impressed by his firm response under that type of pressure. Karl himself tried to avoid any eye contact with the Hauptmann, mostly staring straight ahead and leaning over ever so slightly to hide behind one of the taller recruits in front of him. He surely didn't want to be made a spectacle of.

Hauptmann Mauer stepped back from the lectern, pausing, his arms folded behind his back. Everyone in the room continued to watch his every move, trying to read his face, wondering what would come next. Even Karl peeked up slightly at him. Then the Hauptmann again stepped toward the podium. His words bellowed through the hall: "All now! Repeat after me this time, as loudly as you can and all together!

"I… swear… to… fight… and… defend… my… Vaterland… until… my… death!" Mauer emphasized every word in the sentence.

The boys responded loud and clear this time, almost in perfect unison, adding emphasis to each word and moving their lips as much as they could:

"I swear to fight and defend my Vaterland until my death!"

The sound of three hundred young men shouting the coordinated response echoed inside and outside the large majestic SS hall. Mauer nodded, barely noticeable, pressing his lips together. He was satisfied this time. He responded with an excited "Heil Hitler!", again giving the sharp salute with his stubby arm, and the boys mirrored his action.

"You are now officially indoctrinated into the *Jugend Panzer Division*, the youth tank division!" he announced.

The boys kept their eyes on the Hauptmann, expecting to hear more. Some stood with their mouths wide open, not daring to look at each other, hoping to find more answers. What would come next?

Hauptmann Mauer glanced impatiently at the large clock hanging in the center of the white wall at the far end of the room and continued in a lower voice.

"It is now 11:30. You have exactly twenty-five minutes to go to the mess hall and eat. This will be your last hot meal for a while. At 11:55 you will line up outside the main entrance. At 12:05 sharp you will board trucks that will take you to your destination. If you are not there, expect severe punishment."

Mauer paused and scanned the crowd, attempting to make eye contact with each of the boys. He lowered his voice even more, so everyone had to strain their ears to hear.

"…Don't even think about trying to run. If you do, we will find you no matter where, I promise you. Not only will we track you down, but we will also find your families."

Karl felt everyone holding their breath. He knew threatening the boys with hunting down their families was one of the best ways to scare them into obedience. He felt his stomach sink. At that point, most everyone's father, brother, even grandfather or uncle was either still fighting or dead, and it was the women—mothers, sisters, aunts and grandmothers—who were left behind and the most vulnerable.

The threat ensured that none of the young recruits would dare walk out any back door or try to escape in any way, perhaps on the way to their destination. They would do everything they could to keep their families safe.

Mauer repeated, "Be there at 12:05 sharp! You will form two lines. Hauptmann Bertrandt is in charge of all of you. Supporting him are SS-Scharführer Albert Wüst and SS-Scharführer Manuel Müller. Follow their orders!"

He pointed at Hauptmann Bertrandt, another stubby soldier in his forties, and then at the two Scharführers, Manuel and Albert, both thin and barely eighteen, standing proudly next to the lectern for their introduction. They energetically saluted Hauptmann Mauer, who in turn quickly saluted them back.

"Heil Hitler! Heil, heil, heil!" was the chant with which Mauer ended his speech, slowly moving his chubby arm back and forth with each 'Heil'.

The boys did their best to chime along. The halls echoed, "Heil, heil, heil!"

As swiftly as the Hauptmann had appeared, he disappeared out the large hall side door with his entourage. The doors slammed shut with a loud boom that echoed through the hall.

Karl and Hans, along with the large group of freshly indoctrinated SS soldiers, turned to each other, and soon the questions were flying. "All to the mess hall now, *aber schnell!*" Albert screamed, putting a stop to the slight mayhem. He pointed in the direction of the cafeteria. "We don't have much time! *Marsch, marsch!*" He continued to push everyone down the long hall.

One after the other, they streamed into the hall. They lined up to grab bowls of steaming hot beef soup served from large aluminum pots that sat on the long tables along the stucco wall of the mess hall. All three hundred recruits lined up, waiting to be fed. Karl doubted they all would get to eat before they had to be outside to pile onto the waiting trucks.

"Form two lines, one from the back and one from the front," ordered SS-Scharführer Albert. "Grab your plates and spoons here!" He pointed at the aluminum bowls, plates and spoons stacked neatly on a table at the entrance of the mess hall.

With large soup ladles, enlisted soldiers rationed the soup to one youth at a time, as fast as they could serve.

"Next! Next!" they said after each serving was splattered into the bowls. Further down a Private scooped out potatoes using large ladles from two separate pots.

When it was finally their turn, Hans took both the soup and the potatoes. Karl, who was behind Hans, asked, "What is that?" pointing at the steam rising from the pile resembling food on his brother's plate.

"Not sure. Potatoes, I think. I am so hungry I'll eat anything right now," Hans mumbled back.

"Move along!" the server barked.

Karl decided to have only the soup. "Soup please." And soup was poured into his bowl. He had always been the pickier eater.

"Karl, now is no time to be picky about potatoes. You need to eat anything they offer you," the ever-protective Hans advised, as they looked for a place to sit. Karl just mumbled something and ignored the good intentions of his older brother.

The pair plopped down on the first empty seats they could find next to each other, on one of the crowded benches lined up parallel to the wooden dinner tables throughout the mess hall. They were hungry; this was the first meal they'd had since they were taken from home. And they ate it as fast as they could. Some of the soldiers were already starting to head toward the exit as others were still waiting in line to get their food.

"I wonder if they will have time to eat." Karl mused, nodding in the direction of the long line of waiting recruits.

Hans waved it away. "Nothing we can do about it. They are serving it as fast as they can."

Karl kept picking at his soup. "If this is our last warm meal for a while, I hate to see what the food will be like where we are going. There is hardly any beef in the soup. It's more flavored water than anything," Karl complained.

Hans looked at Karl in disbelief. "You are really going to be this picky? Food won't be like Mutter's here; get used to it!"

Karl forced himself to eat the watery broth. His brother was right, this was no time to be selective; and there might not be another meal offered for a long time. He wondered how they would eat, wherever they were going. Food was already so scarce.

"Hurry up," Karl said to Hans as his older brother shoved in his few last bites of the tasteless potato dish. Many more of the soldiers were now leaving the mess hall, while only a few remained in the food line. When Hans and Karl finally rushed out, many of the recruits had already lined up inside the main exit. Everyone was anxious to get to where they were supposed to be going.

"Form two lines!" SS-Scharführer Albert was ordering, motioning with his outstretched arms at two parallel lines to his left and right. "*Gefreiter* Schenk! Tell everyone in the *Kantine* to come out now!" Albert screamed the order at a dark-haired soldier standing in the far back.

Hans and Karl looked at each other. Yes, some would go hungry on this new journey.

"The line to the right will go to Linz with me, and the line to the left will go to Steg with Scharführer Müller. *Schnell, schnell!*"

Karl's eyes widened with the realization. They were going to Austria! Karl had heard of the two cities in Austria located in the Alps very close to each other.

"One hundred and fifty men on each side!" Albert continued, gesturing to the first youth in line. "Count down, you start! One, two..."

Karl and Hans squeezed into the same line on the right to make sure they would end up going to Linz together. Not only were they making sure they were honoring one of Mutter's last requests to look out for each other, but Hans naturally felt protective of his little brother. He promised himself he would make sure Karl did not ever have to be alone on this journey.

It was Karl's turn to count "130" and then Hans "131". The last few soldiers behind them, and all those who trailed in from the mess hall finished up counting to 150 on each side. A few soldiers had to switch lines to make it an even 150. Each side was then told to exit through their respective doors, right or left.

Outside, soldiers who were part of the organized inductee effort directed the new recruits towards the connecting brick building where each would pick up their *Maschinenpistolen* 40. They had learned to shoot rifles during many of their Hitler Youth exercises; now it was time to learn how to use a machine gun. The trucks idling on the side of the cobblestone road were parked in convoy, ready to take them to their shooting range. The recruits were given the afternoon to practice.

As many of the young soldiers as could fit squeezed into the cab of each of the trucks. Before the trucks took off, Albert and his counterparts checked off a list with the recruits' names and marked each name with their respective truck number. It was their way of keeping inventory of all the soldiers-to-be. Then the trucks drove them to the shooting range.

At the range, each recruit was taught how to use their machine gun—how to load, aim, and shoot. They were instructed to practice on various targets set up in the distance. Then, after a few hours of introductory training, they were herded back onto the trucks to be transported to their final destination.

It was a bumpy but mostly quiet three-hour ride to Linz, and they couldn't see outside. The young men were huddled together, trying to keep each other warm on that cold October day. There was no heat in the back, and nobody talked. They were all too tired and cold, some still hungrier than others, and the realization had settled in that their fate was now in the hands of the SS.

Hans fell asleep to the continuous humming sound of the truck's diesel engine, rumbling down the country roads. In deep slumber, his head fell over onto his little brother's shoulder. The last couple of days had been exhausting for all of them.

Karl looked across at the other soldiers sitting against the wall as his mind wandered.

How long will we be in Linz? What will we do there? There is no fighting front, at least not yet. Or is the enemy that close? He had heard the Russians were closing in, but he didn't think they were already in Linz.

The thoughts kept piling on until, after a while, the exhaustion caught up with him, and Karl also fell asleep. His head nodded over on top of his brother's head, nestled snugly on Hans' shoulder.

****

"Wake up! We are here!" Karl woke to Alois, the soldier sitting on the right side of him, shaking his shoulder.

Karl, in turn, nudged his brother who was still asleep. "We are here. We need to get off."

One by one, the recruits jumped off the truck. The sun was setting already, and in less than thirty minutes it would be dark. Everyone lined up quickly.

Albert had already begun barking orders at them. "We need to set up the tents! Grab the poles and tents over there! Then also take a spade from those trucks over there." Albert pointed toward two trucks parked on the side of a graveled road.

"I'll hand the spades down!" one of the young recruits eagerly volunteered, running toward the truck.

How can he have this much energy? Karl wondered in amazement. The soldier's name was Anton Walter—he had sat next to Karl in the mess hall. They had had a brief introduction and a small exchange discussing their blood types.

A gunshot echoed through the cold mountain air. The baffled young SS stopped mid-run and reflexively covered his head. Startled, Karl looked in the direction of the shot. Albert had fired his rifle into the air.

"You are not to do anything unless I order you to do so!" he angrily screamed at Anton. "Get back in line!"

"Yes, sir!" Red-faced and shaken, Anton trotted back into the line.

"*Schütze* Milz there on the back of the truck will hand down the tent poles and the spades." Albert motioned to the soldier standing near the truck. "Now, *one by one,* all of you go over there and pick up your tools!"

The young SS soldiers, some more eager to help out than others, each lined up to grab the equipment.

Under Albert's instruction, the young troops pitched their tents. Then it was time to start digging the trenches.

"They each will need to be about five hundred meters long, two meters wide, and about a meter and a half deep!"

Albert gestured with his rifle to where they were to dig, pointing the rifle up and down and sideways: "A thousand meters along here should stop some of the tanks."

He shouldn't be swinging a loaded rifle like that. Karl felt his irritation for Albert returning.

He scanned the brown grass fields covering wide open space. Far off in the distance, he could just make out the edge of a forest against the majestic Alps. The air was crisp, and the sky had a pink hue from the setting sun. There was only a light breeze—they were lucky there was no snow yet. Only the mountain caps were covered in snow. It had been a mild October so far.

Karl knew that since they were near Linz, they were very close to the Eastern border. Czechoslovakia was only about three hours away from where the Russians were moving in.

"Line up and start digging now!" screamed Albert.

"It's getting dark," Karl tried to protest.

"Stop complaining! You still have at least twenty minutes of daylight. Get going!"

"*Auf,* let's get started!" Hans mumbled in a resigned tone to his brother.

"You'd better, and fast!" Albert seemed specifically interested in Karl and Hans' interactions and never missed a word, no matter how quietly they tried to communicate.

"We don't have much time!" Albert went on, seething at the entire group now. "The Russians are not that far away; they are closing in! This is just one of the many trenches we'll dig to stop them from getting any further! They will have to roll over my dead body before I let a single tank get through under my watch! Get to work now, *aber schnell!"*

With their foldable spades in hand, Karl and Hans walked over to line up next to the other soldiers who had already started digging on each side of the five-meter-wide space destined to become part of a trench. The wind was picking up, and Karl felt a chill despite his woolen jacket.

They all got to work, stomping their boots on their spades and using all their strength to dig as deep into the ground as they could.

Karl's first stomp only dug into the first layer of grass and some dirt. The ground was cold and hard, and didn't want to budge. He moved a couple steps to the side to find softer ground. When he pushed the spade in again with his boot, it dug a bit deeper. Then Karl decided to stand on the spade with both his boots, and putting his full weight onto it, he jumped up and down on the spade.

Slowly, the dirt made way. Because of the recent milder temperatures, it was still possible to dig; but soon the ground would be entirely frozen and very difficult to work with. It became clear this digging would be a strenuous process.

A few more trucks of soldiers arrived, and soon all one hundred and fifty of the new SS soldiers were lined up and working on digging the tank trenches, though it was getting so dark they could hardly see.

"Time to wrap up! Keep your spades with you. They are part of you now, along with your machine guns!" Albert ordered. "You are responsible for them. If you lose them, you won't get them back. There are no replacements, and you will be stuck here without any tools or a weapon!"

Their first day as indoctrinated SS had come to an end. Tired and hungry, the recruits retired to their sturdy tents and quickly fell asleep.

The digging resumed early the next morning. One spade of dirt was heaped onto the next as the arduous, tedious task continued, minute after minute, hour after hour. When the sun began to beat down from directly above them, and after what seemed an eternity of laboring away, Hans heard some of the soldiers near him beginning to complain. "I need a break," one said.

Another added, "I am thirsty!" and they both sat down on the ground, laying their spades next to them.

Albert was on them immediately. "You get a break at noon," he hissed. "*Mach weiter,* keep going! Get up!"

The soldiers grumbled, but slowly got up to continue digging.

"*Mensch,* I am also thirsty," Karl whispered to Hans. "I wonder how much longer it is until noon." Neither had the luxury of having a watch.

Hans responded, keeping his voice down, "Judging by the sun's location, it must be close to noon. Thirty minutes or so?"

"I am not sure I can make it that long," Karl replied. He was dehydrated and exhausted. Sweat was pooling on his forehead, and he wiped it away with the back of his hand.

Both were feeling weak from eating so little in the past forty-eight hours. When Albert walked by to oversee the progress up and down the trench, Karl whispered so only Albert could hear: "You should at least allow people to drink water! Everybody is thirsty. How often did you drink water and eat for free at our house?"

That was the first reference Karl made to Albert about their common childhood memories since Albert's radicalized transformation. Growing up, Albert had spent more time at their house than at his own, because he loved Mutter's cooking.

Albert looked at Karl for a few seconds in utter disbelief, as if pondering how to respond to Karl, who had dared to bring up the past to him, the senior rank in charge. With eyes still fixed on Karl, Albert yelled an order at a soldier working fifty meters away: "Lance Corporal Schenk! Come here!"

The soldier near the spade truck, who pretended not to have noticed the interaction, but had been watching it intensely all along, quickly marched toward Albert.

"*Jawohl,* Herr SS-Scharführer?" he asked Albert eagerly, saluting.

"Gefreiter Schenk, when can you be ready to give everyone water?"

"Herr SS-Scharführer, I am ready now. I can take each of their water containers and fill it with water." He gestured toward the water cisterns on the back of a truck. He had filled it with fresh water from the nearby creek that snaked through the mountains.

"All right, then, the soldiers here are thirsty and tired. Get them water now!" ordered Albert.

"*Jawohl,* Herr SS-Scharführer!" Schenk immediately saluted, half-grinning. He clicked his heels, turned around quickly and marched toward the water truck. He seemed ready to do his share to support the troops. In no time he returned with the containers filled with water.

"*Hier*!" he handed the water container to the first soldier in line. "Drink and pass it down!"

As the soldiers drank, Lance Corporal Schenk ran back and forth, handing back the containers and instructing everyone to pass them down.

Karl reached out his hand to signal he still didn't have any water. Only a few steps away, Albert stepped over and grabbed a container from the corporal and then marched back to Karl.

"Thank you," Karl said, giving Albert a grateful look as he accepted the container. After he had gulped his first sips, he gave the container to Hans, standing right next to him: "Here, drink!" Parched, Hans eagerly grabbed it and gulped it as if he had been stranded in a desert for days, drooling water down the side of his mouth. It was almost empty when he handed it back to Karl. "Finish!" he said, and Karl downed the rest.

"Ahhhh! Much better!" Schenk had approached them, and now grabbed the empty water container, handing Karl the full one in his other hand. "Here."

"*Vielen Dank*, thanks." Karl very much appreciated the accommodating gesture from Lance Corporal Schenk, who didn't look much older than Karl. *He's eighteen at most.*

"What about you? Did you get anything to drink?" Karl offered the water back to the young corporal.

"I am good!" He waved the water away.

Albert stood nearby, silently watching the entire interaction.

"Back to work now, boys!" he ordered everyone after all had had their share of water.

Appeased, Karl and Hans and the rest of the soldiers continued the arduous task of digging the trenches. Karl was slightly relieved at seeing this somewhat better side of Albert. He hadn't punished him for reminding him of their youth together.

Hans had been very close in guessing the time, as forty minutes later, at noon, they were given a twenty-minute break and were ordered to pick up their food rations: cooked but now-cold potatoes, red apples, and one slice of bread each, along with some more water.

The rations were supposed to be delivered by truck from field kitchens to all the locations where the different groups of soldiers were located. It was also supposed to be kept warm in thermos containers.

But often the trucks arrived late or not at all. And when they finally did get a new truckload of food, by the time it was fed to the young soldiers, it was almost always cold.

Someone mentioned not wanting to build a fire to heat it up because the smoke would have been visible for kilometers, giving away their location.

"How close is the enemy really?" Karl asked. Everyone knew the Russians were closing in, but the question of how close still remained. Nobody answered, but Karl had a feeling it would not be long before the enemy was here. He finished eating his stale bread in silence.

After the break, they continued to dig until dark. Finally, at 17:00, they were told to stop because it was nearly impossible to see, and they all once again crawled exhausted into their crowded tents.

It was the second of many freezing nights they would endure while here digging trenches. At night, the temperature dropped down to minus-five degrees Celsius. They were short on blankets, so Karl and Hans ended up sleeping with their winter coats and gloves on.

The next morning, Albert woke them up by hitting large spoons against one of the tin pots. He was banging as loudly as he could, taking too much pleasure in waking the workers in such a spiteful way. Then he ordered his young troop to stand in formation.

"We will also need guards for the area, day and night!" he bellowed at them.

"You will take turns! Two pairs of guards at a time, four hours each! You'll take turns in alphabetical order and by age. We start with the oldest ones in this group first."

"Aachen, Acker, Almen, and Bach," he read off the list in his hand. "Step forward!"

The soldiers stepped forward: "Heil Hitler!"

Albert was opening his mouth to bellow more orders when air raid sirens suddenly screeched from nearby Linz, loud enough to be heard many kilometers away.

"Air attack!" someone screamed.

Everyone frantically looked around, unsure of what to do. There was nothing but wide-open field. No buildings, no bunkers to hide in.

"Run to the trench!" Hans ordered Karl as he dashed to the nearest trench. "Run!" As Karl broke into a run after him, a few soldiers followed them. Others didn't move at all, frozen with fear.

Over the ruckus, Karl heard Albert screaming, "Grab all your guns! All of you. We want to prepare to shoot at the planes if they fly over us!"

"Get your weapons!" he screamed again, at the soldiers nearest to him. "Get in the trench, but have the guns ready and pointed at whatever comes at us!"

Another group of five soldiers in the distance frantically readied the *Fliegerabwehrkanone,* the only aircraft defense canon the group had available to them. They rolled it into place, but then didn't know in which direction to point it. There was nothing but blue horizon and white clouds to be seen in the skies.

The sirens kept blaring, its decibel levels moving up and down. Karl couldn't believe Albert was telling them to use their machine guns—machine guns couldn't shoot down a plane. It would have to be flying incredibly low for that to be remotely effective. Albert had never been the smartest in class, but surely the Hitler Youth or common sense would have taught him that?

"Everyone lay flat in the trench! Down!" Karl shouted as instinct kicked in.

"You are not in charge!" Albert responded angrily, though Karl could see it written on Albert's face that he himself was out of ideas. "We can't defend ourselves, Albert!"

Then, as suddenly as it had started, the sirens ceased, and there was complete silence. The soldiers who were still running around frantically stopped in their tracks. Everyone listened, leery of the eerie silence. Karl and Hans strained their ears for the faintest sounds of a plane, scanning the skies far into the distance. There was nothing.

A false alarm, maybe? They continued to cautiously scout the skies for a bit longer.

Karl broke the silence, moving closer to Albert so only he would hear. "Albert, we need a plan to be better prepared for air attacks! What is everyone to do when we are attacked from above? We need a place to hide, and it can't be out in the open like this!"

Agitated, Albert immediately snapped back, "We only have one anti-aircraft cannon for the entire group. We have machine guns and not nearly enough ammunition! *Feldwebel* Bertrandt has requested more ammunition, tanks, anti-aircraft support, everything for us! But the soldiers on the fronts need more weapons to hold off the enemy. We are here to dig trenches. We are given spades. We have no rockets, and we have nothing! What is your plan, Karl? You are in this as much as I am. So you tell me, what should we do?"

Albert got really close to Karl's face, his frustration pouring out. Karl stared back at Albert in disbelief. In that moment, Karl felt he could read Albert's soul, and sensed how helpless he felt.

Albert was scared.

"The enemy is much closer, isn't he?" asked Hans, who was standing nearby.

Albert looked away and didn't respond.

"How close, Albert? How close?"

Albert looked down. Quietly, resigned, he responded, "I am not one hundred percent sure how close, but yes, the Russians are very close. I think they might be within a hundred kilometers. Or even closer."

Hans looked at Karl as if to say, can you believe this? Karl shrugged his shoulders in response, shaking his head.

Hans turned back to Albert. "And you think those mole holes we are digging are going to keep the Russians away?" he scoffed.

They all knew the answer.

Albert continued to avoid eye contact with the brothers, his eyes glued to his feet. "The trenches will keep them away for at least a day or so," he muttered. "They will have to go around and find another way to get to their destination. They are heading for Berlin."

Hans shook his head. "We have lost the war."

He turned to Karl. "With the Russians this close coming from the east and the Americans and other Allies coming from the west, it is practically over,"

"Let us not give up yet." Albert tried and failed to sound convincing. It was almost like the old days, when Albert, Hans, and Karl were in their old neighborhood, planning and scheming how to quickly traverse the farmer's forbidden large wheat field without getting lost. Forgotten for a moment was Albert's rank in this SS troop. They were all standing together, realizing that the war was nearly over. Germany had been defeated. Hitler had lied and continued to lie to the entire country. They had been led by a lunatic into a deadly, unwinnable war. How devastating it had been for their home country, as they had to watch it all unfold helplessly and now had been dragged into it against their will.

"Enough of that!" Albert jumped back as if stung by a wasp. "I am in charge here!" He stormed toward the rest of the soldiers that were scattered throughout the area in separate groups all puzzling about their fate after the false air raid alarm.

Albert screamed as loud as possible for everyone to get back into formation. He didn't address the sirens or what they should do when there was another imminent air raid. Instead, he continued his earlier orders. He had no solution. An air attack would be deadly for all the soldiers there out in the wide-open space of the green fields, mapped against the Alps.

"We need to guard the area with an eight-kilometer perimeter, two kilometers on each side. You are to cover the marked area for four hours, armed with your machine guns."

"What should we do when there is another air attack warning?" the pimple-faced soldier named Bach piped up. Karl recognized him as the same soldier who had been called out by Hauptmann Mauer, back at the SS headquarters.

Albert squinted his eyes at the young SS. For a split second, he looked as if he were deciding what to do about this young soldier's disrespect and interruption mid-order. But he continued without regarding the misbehavior, even more irritation in his voice.

"When your guard time is up, after the four hours, switch with the next four guards in line. We are setting up a roster." He repeated the names he had shouted out just before the false alarm: "Aachen, Acker, Almen, Bach!"

"You two go this direction," he directed Aachen and Acker to his right, toward the north, "and we will go east." He looked at the soldiers Almen and Bach. "We will meet halfway."

"Mark each kilometer as a milestone, so you know how far you have gone. Try to step out one meter at a time, count to a thousand and then mark the one kilometer with a thick stick."

"*Jawohl,* SS-Scharführer!" the newly appointed guards responded in unison.

Then Albert turned back to the rest of the troop standing in formation. "While I am gone, Gefreiter Schenk is in charge! You listen to his orders! Gefreiter Schenk knows to go to Feldwebel Betrandt if needed."

"… And one last thing: If there is another air raid warning, seek shelter in the trenches! Our machine guns won't stand a chance against the planes. It's best just to hide."

Karl and Hans looked at each other knowingly. Albert had actually paid attention to them and was trying to make sense after all. They all knew the end was near. What the end would look like and whether they would survive it were some of the questions they asked themselves each day.

"Let's go!" Albert gestured to his guards, and they marched off toward the east as the other pair marched north.

"Count 1, 2 …" With each large step, Corporal Bach measured each approximate meter. After roughly a thousand meters, Albert instructed them to mark the corners with a small tree branch.

As they marched along, Albert started to sing.

"Trust no Fox on his Green Heath

And no Jew with our girls…"

It was a play on words based on the famous Nazi children's book. Back home, Albert had overheard some of the SS claiming that Jews were taking their girlfriends away.

Nobody joined Albert in his idiotic rhyme, but he didn't seem to care as he continued to sing the racist song.

Back at camp, the soldiers continued digging the trenches. And when night set in, Karl and Hans crawled into their tents, still wearing their winter coats to protect them from the chill. They huddled next to each other and settled in for yet another uneventful night at camp. Exhausted from the full day of hard labor, they quickly fell asleep. Digging the trenches became their daily routine. The ground got increasingly harder as the time went on and winter set in. It often snowed, and then there was no progress at all, or it was slow at best. The days also grew shorter; much of the soldiers' time was spent in the tents, just passing the time playing the popular card game Skat, or writing letters that would never be sent on rare scraps of paper, or talking and daydreaming while trying to stay warm.

Morning, lunch, and dinner they were fed the same food: apples, cold potatoes, and sometimes pears; but rarely any meat, and never any warm food. They were told the food trucks were very delayed, even for the soldiers at the front. They were running out of food.

Will we starve to death? Karl often wondered.

After two months on the field, Feldwebel Bertrandt informed them in a harsh tone that the front was closing in and that the German fighters were being forced to retreat further and further back. The front was now only fifty or so kilometers away, they were told, and it needed their help more than ever. Realizing how young some of these boys were, Feldwebel Bertrandt asked first for volunteers. But Albert handpicked the oldest soldiers from his troop—they didn't have any say in it.

Hans was one of the soldiers called to join the fight at the front, and immediately Karl also volunteered. He could not imagine letting his brother fight alone. Albert didn't object. He had known that if Hans went that Karl would insist on going also.

"Anyone who volunteers to go to the front to fight won't be denied the opportunity," he mused.

They were transported fifty kilometers east. When they finally got to the designated spot, they were handed heavy helmets and told to immediately dig in next to the soldiers who had already made their dugouts. This time, in order to protect them from view, the trenches were deep enough that they could almost stand in them. But they were still told to duck and to keep their heads down.

As darkness settled, they could see fire being exchanged in the near distance, farther east. To Karl, it looked like fireworks. The Russians were still too far away for the German group to directly come under fire, but he could hear the Russians soldiers singing and celebrating, because they knew the Germans were retreating and they were winning the war.

Karl knew that the advancing Russians pilfered the German farmers' alcohol and food, but their drunkenness and thievery was nothing compared to the other atrocities he heard about.

The next day, in the very early daylight, while trotting back to his dugout from grabbing a few potatoes, Karl noticed a familiar-looking soldier passing by.

"Wait!" He reached for the soldier's arm to get his attention and to look directly at him. "Aren't you—"

Facing him now, Karl recognized the startled soldier immediately. The name embroidered on the soldier's nametag further confirmed Karl's suspicions.

"*You!*" Karl exclaimed. "Gefreiter Ferdinand! You came with Albert that night! You took my brother, Hermann!"

Ferdinand's face had lost all its color, and he looked petrified. Karl was fuming, ready to leap at Ferdinand.

"Where is he? Where did you take him?"

"He is home!"

"What do you mean he is home?" Karl was taken aback. This was not the response he had expected. He frantically tried to read Ferdinand's green eyes to see whether he was telling the truth, ready to attack him at the same time. They were out in the middle of nowhere at the front, soon to be shot at and highly likely killed— Karl had no qualms about what he wanted to do to this fellow soldier. And that was very clear to Ferdinand by Karl's demeanor. Ferdinand spoke fast: "You have to believe me! Hermann is home! Albert wanted me to bring Hermann to a camp near München, it's called Dachau—or something like that—and apparently, a lot of cripples are sent there. But why drive two hours for a handicapped boy who can't do any work or support the fatherland in any way? I just didn't have time for that!

"So, once Albert and you all were out of sight, I just got Hermann out of the car and wheeled him back into your house. It would have been such a waste of my time. I am here to support the war and win it, not do useless, time-consuming work!"

Karl was baffled. It still sounded unbelievable. An SS doesn't defy orders!

As if reading Karl's mind, Ferdinand quickly elaborated. "Albert should have never insisted we take anyone in a wheelchair, but I pretended to do it to appease him. I didn't want to disagree with him. Albert has a terrible temper!"

"But how can I believe that you took my brother back?" As much as Karl wanted to, he could not bring himself to believe Ferdinand's story. He took a step closer towards the soldier.

"I am telling the truth! I really brought your brother back home the same night, I swear!" The words were frantically pouring out of Ferdinand's mouth as he cowered away from Karl. *What is he still hiding?* Karl wanted to know.

Getting very close to his face, Karl spoke to Ferdinand in a low, threatening tone. "I know Albert has a terrible temper. So aren't you worried you will get caught?"

"I knew Albert would leave the next day—he had orders to go to Linz to lead you guys! I knew he wouldn't have had time to track down what happened to Hermann. He had bigger things to worry about and…"—Ferdinand paused and lowered his voice—"…he trusts me!" He looked down as if ashamed that he had abused that trust.

Ferdinand's story was beginning to sound more convincing, and Karl started to hope more and more that he was telling the truth. But he remained skeptical.

"What did Mutter do when you brought him back that night?" Karl squinted his eyes at Ferdinand.

"She was ecstatic. She hugged me over and over and even insisted I take a handful of potatoes." Ferdinand smiled as he recalled it. Handing out some of their potatoes was something Mutter would do. That was one of her trademarks—handing out potatoes or apples or other small food items to the kids who accompanied their customers, even though there often wasn't enough for them. When questioned by Opa, who was often irritated by such a generous gesture, Mutter's response had been that they could always grow more potatoes.

"Don't ever let Albert find out!" Ferdinand whispered desperately. "He will probably have me shipped off to that camp Dachau himself if he does. The war is over soon, and nobody will care anymore, but until then he just can't know."

Karl nodded. He would not say anything to the brainwashed Albert. His anger at Albert had been rekindled. How dare he order Hermann to a camp? What kind of camp was it, anyhow? Hermann couldn't do any work. Albert would pay for this!

Karl felt like strangling him. *Maybe in his tent while he was asleep one night...* The thought flashed across Karl's mind, and he entertained it for a moment. But then he quickly shook it away. He was not a murderer.

Instead, Karl left Ferdinand and ran toward where he had last seen Hans holed up in the dugout.

"Hermann is supposedly at home with Mutter and Opa!" he whispered urgently.

Hans' eyes grew wide. "What do you mean? How do you know?"

Karl retold Ferdinand's story, confirming that he hadn't believed

Ferdinand either, at first. But then he had told about Mutter offering potatoes as a reward, and that part of the story made sense. Hans and Karl started to believe it could be true. They wanted it to be true. They needed some happy news.

"Where is Gefreiter Ferdinand now?" Hans wanted to hear it from him directly and look the other soldier in the eyes as he told it. Was he really telling the truth? Or was he just appeasing Karl?

Suddenly, gunfire erupted in the near distance. The shots were getting louder and closer. Using their foldable spades, the soldiers rapidly dug deeper and wider for better protection from direct gunfire. But they were still not safe from aircraft fire or hand grenades.

Their fear of dying needlessly for a war they didn't believe in grew larger by the hour. Karl prayed quietly, pleading with God, "Please let me get back home safely to my family. Please let them be alright."

He spotted someone running towards their dugout. "There is Ferdinand!" he shouted.

A salvo of shots hit the group very close to them, and Ferdinand was hit from behind. He fell ten feet in front of Karl. He was dead when he hit the ground. Ferdinand and six other soldiers lost their lives that day.

****

After a few hours the attack began to die down. The ever-so-slight possibility of Hermann being back home returned to Karl and Hans' minds, improving their morale. But having to remain focused on yet another imminent attack was physically demanding and exhausting; over the next few days, they got little sleep, often sleeping while half standing or half kneeling. They never wanted to lie down completely, always having the machine gun propped up and ready. They were beyond fatigued, dirty, and constantly hungry. They had no protection from the elements—wind, rain, and that evening it was even snowing. They were always cold, and the days of pure sunshine and calm were rare. A few of their fellow soldiers even suffered from frostbite. Their food was rationed further: two potatoes in the morning, watery potato or sugar beet soup at lunch, stale bread for dinner, and a few apples in between.

One day they were given unripe green apples, and that night many of the soldiers, including Karl and Hans, ended up with painful diarrhea. Having the runs was even more difficult to manage in the dark with no latrine nearby, while seeing 'fireworks' that could kill them in the near distance. That night, Karl cursed his fate, the universe, and swore off green apples forever.

Over a week had passed with them holed up in the front trenches, when another group of thirty soldiers who had retreated from further east joined them. All German troops were now in retreat, and this additional group that had joined them was digging in near them. The new batch of soldiers was much older, and with one look at Albert's youngsters, as they called them, Hauptmann Schwabe, who was in charge, refused to work with them.

"I am not going to be responsible for these kids! Send them back to where they came from. My troop has this covered!"

What a wonderful man! Karl thought. Schwabe completely disregarded Hitler's insane order that young teenage boys should be fighting at the front, giving their lives. Someone said he had two sons their age, neither of whom he had heard from in years. "Go back to digging trenches!" he insisted.

Without any complaints, Karl and Hans and the rest of the youths in Albert's troop were trucked back fifty kilometers. Within a few days, they were joined by the rest of the recruits they had parted with back in Nürnberg, after they had been tattooed. Three hundred recruits were now digging within ten kilometers of Linz.

Karl was glad to be in a somewhat safer environment. He would not have to volunteer for the front again, nor could Albert force Hans or any of them to go again. But what would it mean to be in a safe environment these days? They weren't under direct attack right now, but Karl knew that it would be only a matter of time before the Allied Forces would arrive there too.

The December nights and days became copies of each other. It often snowed, and the young soldiers were always very cold. Karl had long since stopped keeping track of what day of the week it was. He would have missed Christmas completely if someone hadn't mentioned it.

They were not allowed to officially celebrate this most important religious holiday. So in silence, Karl and Hans prayed longer than they ever had before. Karl reminisced about how before the war started, Uncle Joseph and Opa cut the Christmas pine tree for the house and set it up in the living room corner, tied by a rope to the wall, and how Mutter and the boys decorated it with real clip-on, white wax candles and sparklers. The candles would be lit and reused every year until only stumps were left.

He thought about how they would sing *Silent Night* around the Christmas tree with those candles burning on it, until one Christmas the tree caught fire. Uncle Joseph had used blankets to extinguish the fire—a Christmas they would never forget for all the wrong reasons. But that day during the war, when no religious displays were allowed, Christmas came and went as just any other day. Karl felt homesick.

For months they continued the routine of laboring away at the ravines, moving inland as one trench after the other was finished. They had dug acres and acres of trenches.

Soon, it was March, and some of the field flowers were starting to bloom: crocuses, daffodils and forget-me-nots could be seen in the distance. One of Mutter's favorite flowers was the forget-me-not, Karl mused. She would grow them in her garden, and they would bloom in the spring and fall.

One day, during their routine digging, Karl heard laughter nearby, growing louder and louder. He paused his digging to look up and see what the ruckus was about.

Some of the laughing soldiers were pointing at two guards walking back toward camp, returning from their guard duty.

The young guards were Bach and Milz. Karl had seen them leave with their weapons—they had been almost dragging the rifles on the ground, being the youngest and shortest in the group. But now they were without their machine guns. And their pants were cut off. Karl put his spade down and walked toward the crowd of soldiers that now surrounded the young boys.

"What happened? Who did that to you?" Albert came storming toward the two boys at the center of the nosy crowd. He inspected them as if to make sure they were not hurt.

Bach responded with tears of frustration streaming down his dirty face. "The Russians!" he exclaimed, pointing to where they came from, and then he just looked down in embarrassment. Everyone looked east in the direction Bach was pointing, but there was nothing to be seen but flowered fields up until the forest tree line in the far distance.

Milz explained further: "We walked just a bit past the four-kilometer marker. I know we shouldn't have, but we wanted to find mushrooms in the forest. *Pfifferlinge* are my favorite, and I figured we'd find many inside the forest."

Albert interrupted him angrily. "Pfifferlinge won't grow until late summer!" He, Karl, Hans, and Daniel often went to collect those mushrooms in their nearby woods. *Steinpilze* was their favorite. They would sometimes spend hours in the forest searching for them. The excellent taste of fried Pfifferlinge and Steinpilze scrambled with eggs was the delicious reward.

For a minute, Milz was sidetracked on whether his favorite mushroom was in season yet. "Are you sure?" he countered Albert. But then he shook his head and continued. "After a few steps inside the forest, out of nowhere, two Russian soldiers appeared. I could not tell their rank. They were in their thirties. They tried to talk to us, but we don't speak Russian, and they don't speak German. I froze. I couldn't even use the rifle; it happened so fast. They pointed their machine guns at us. They pushed us to get down and one took out his knife—I thought he wanted to kill us. I thought this is the end. I was looking up in the sky just waiting for them to cut my throat." At this Milz also started crying. He was just a young boy.

Bach had regained enough composure to pick up where Milz left off. "Then they cut and ripped off our pant legs. Nothing else. They were trying to tell us something. They were signaling, I think, to tell everyone here that the Russians won't fight with kids. I could understand him say 'Kinder,' and he waved his hands in disgust, and that's the only German word I understood. Then they yanked our rifles from us and marched away with them. And we ran back as fast as we could."

"How deep in the forest were you? Are you saying they are right there in the forest line passed the fields?" asked Albert, his voice betraying his panic. He pointed at the tree lining just a few kilometers downhill.

"Yes!" Bach and Milz responded in unison.

"Do they know we are here? Were you followed?" Albert continued the inquiry.

"I don't think so. I don't really know..." Bach thought for a moment, then shook his head. "No, they didn't follow us. We kept looking back, but they didn't follow us. They just walked back in the forest, laughing."

"We are sitting ducks out here!" Karl exclaimed, trying to be realistic. "Of course they know we are here!"

Albert turned as white as Karl had ever seen him, and then immediately began bellowing more orders.

"We will march further inland. We have to retreat towards the west." With no objections, the soldiers hurriedly packed up their tents, loaded everything on the trucks, and started the hour-long march inland, to the opposite side of Linz.

When they arrived and quickly again unloaded, Albert began shouting more orders.

"Back to digging the trenches! The Russians are closer than we think. We won't let them get through here!"

Everyone looked at each other and grumbled, unfolding their spades and resuming their digging positions.

"The Russians are already here. It's just a matter of days before they reach us!" Hans said to Karl as they both sank their spades into the ground.

"We have lost the war. It is over. Why are we still doing this?" Karl agreed, incredulous. Hans just shrugged his shoulders, defeated.

"I guess it's not over until Hitler officially surrenders or he is killed. Why can't someone just kill that bastard?"

Nobody heard from or saw those two Russians again. Were those two Russian scouts just by themselves, far away from their troop or battalion? They must have been. The soldiers appeased themselves by thinking it must have been a fluke. The guards were strictly instructed to stick to the newly-outlined eight-kilometer perimeter and to stay far away from any tree line.

Eventually it was once again Hans and Karl's turn at four-hour guard duty, starting at midnight. As part of the routine, the two guards before them would wake up Karl and Hans when they had completed their shift. The brothers went to sleep the night before knowing midnight would be there before they knew it. Exhausted, it took them only minutes to fall asleep.

The guards never came.

When Karl woke up, he saw the sun making its way up on the horizon in all sorts of pink and red hues behind the Alps. He looked around, confused. *Why didn't the guards wake us up? Why didn't they come so we could relieve them?*

Karl stepped outside his tent and looked around. There wasn't any movement around the camp. The rest of the soldiers seemed to be in their tents asleep. He walked over to the tent next door and saw the other pair of guards, who were supposed to join Hans and Karl at midnight, fast asleep. Karl hurried back to his tent and roused his brother.

"Hans, they didn't come and get us!" he whispered.

Hans mumbled something unintelligible and rolled over and went back to sleep. Shaking his head, Karl marched over to Albert's tent, one of the larger tents set up for the higher ranking SSs.

Leaning toward the entrance of the tent, Karl tried to whisper as loud as he could without waking the others, "Albert!" Immediately he heard rustling in the tent.

"What?" Albert stormed to the front of the tent and ripped it open, angered by the disturbance.

"The guards didn't come to get us. They were supposed to come back and get Hans and me at midnight, so we could switch," Karl whispered.

"*Scheisse!* They probably deserted us! Let's go look for them, I'll be right back." Albert disappeared back inside the tent to put on his tattered coat and grab his machine gun.

"Let's get Hans, too," Karl suggested. "Hans can come with us. I also have to get my machine gun."

Albert followed Karl back to his and Hans' tent, where Hans was still asleep.

"Hans, wake up," Karl tried again, shaking his shoulder. "Hans, the guards didn't come to get us. Albert and I are going to look for them."

Hans opened his eyes. "What?"

"The guards are missing!" Karl repeated.

Hans jumped up. "What?"

"We are going to find them," Albert repeated.

"Come with us!" Karl directed Hans.

As he jumped up, Hans grabbed the coat he had been using as a blanket and pulled it on while chasing after Karl and Albert, who were already heading east. As he caught up, Hans noticed Albert and Karl were carrying their machine guns. "I forgot mine."

"I've got you covered," Karl responded shortly.

With that, the three continued to march east along the perimeter. At an altitude of nearly three hundred meters, this early in the morning, the winds were howling and blowing dust into their already cold faces. Though the sunrise was beautiful, emblazoning the entire sky in a bright pink hue, they were walking directly into the rising sun and had to squint through the wind and dust to see ahead of them. They passed the two-kilometer marker with no sight of the guards. When they got to the four-kilometer mark, Hans pointed into the distance, where a bunch of vultures were circling.

"Look!"

Hans started running. Karl and Albert followed close behind.

In the distance, a few flecks of grey and brown could be seen in one of the few pockets of snow plotted throughout the landscape. But the boys couldn't see exactly what it was—they were running directly toward the bright morning sunlight, and fighting the wind.

Karl reached the scene first. He screamed in disbelief. "Is that them? *Mein Gott!*"

The bodies of their comrades were scattered on the ground. Their throats had been slit. Dried blood covered their faces and necks.

"Mein Gott!" Karl repeated, aghast.

The gruesome scene nearly sent the boys into shock. This was only their second time witnessing war casualties, the first being when Ferdinand was shot in front of them. This was just as disturbing, if not more.

Albert immediately ripped his machine gun off his shoulder, aiming it as he moved around, searching for the enemy, ready to shoot. There wasn't a soul to be seen—nothing but empty grass fields, with the howling wind drowning out any other noise.

Karl and Hans joined Albert, and frantically they all scanned the far-distant forest line. Beyond that, it was just acres and acres of deep, thick forest. Anyone could be hiding in the thickness of those tall black pine trees. They were probably being monitored as they stood there.

"Let's get back! We'll warn everyone and get backup." Albert took off, back toward their camp.

"Shouldn't we do something with the bodies?" Hans responded.

Karl nodded, unable to take his eyes off the gruesome sight. "We should bury them."

"They are dead. Do you want to be next? I'll have backup come for them!" Albert shouted over his shoulder.

Resigned, Hans and Karl raced behind Albert. As they ran, they once in a while looked back in the direction of the bodies to see if anyone would appear. The enemy could appear from the tree line at any second.

But there was nothing. Nothing but empty eeriness and the few vultures circling once more.

Chapter 7

Americans

When the trio arrived back at their camp, Albert frantically notified Feldwebel Bertrandt of what they had discovered.

Feldwebel Bertrandt ordered a few of the older soldiers to go back to find the bodies, so they could bury them. To prevent other guards from being murdered, he also ordered everyone to go in groups of four guards now instead of just two, each armed with their machine guns—no longer were they to split up and meet in the middle.

Each soldier was held responsible for keeping his fellows awake during guard duty. Given the recent developments, this wouldn't be a very difficult task.

Since Albert figured the enemy was easier on the younger ones, mostly the youngest of the troop were sent.

They suspected that the two guards had fallen asleep, making them easy prey, but they never were able to recreate the details of what exactly had happened.

Within a few weeks, Karl seemed to have recovered from the shock of seeing his peers with their throats cut. But Hans still had night-terrors. Karl often had to shake him awake in the dead of night when he heard him moaning while tossing and turning. It took a lot of effort to make Hans realize he was just having a really bad dream.

Karl grew more and more discouraged. He was convinced this was all a waste of time, and he didn't see the point of having the guards at all. This entire effort was just a charade to give everyone in their little group the feeling of having some type of control, he was convinced.

The enemy was closing in on them. What were they to do if they were attacked? Karl shrugged his shoulders at the thought of it, knowing how woefully unprepared they were in the face of any type of enemy attack. He knew it was just a matter of days, if not hours before all of this was over. Would he and Hans survive?

They were fighting in a war they didn't believe in, and now they were prisoners in their own country.

The days blended together. On May 8th, 1945—yet another cold early morning in the mountains—the soldiers found themselves once again shoveling dirt pile after dirt pile on top of another, wasting time laboring away at the pointless trenches.

The digging was much easier now that the ground had fully thawed. The cold winter days that they had begun in, when they didn't make any progress digging at all, were long behind them. They were making progress again, and it was giving them a greater sense of purpose.

Regardless, they were still constantly exhausted, cold and hungry. They had been here about seven months now, covering acres and acres of ground. The group had dug a multitude of trenches, tearing up the countryside like gigantic moles. The muscles in their backs constantly ached; their faces were weathered and burned from the relentless wind and cold. Whenever a trench was completed to Albert's satisfaction, they moved further inland—trench by trench, ditch by ditch, farther from the eastern front, from where the enemy was rapidly closing in.

Surely the deep trenches will slow the enemy down, won't they? Karl had tried to convince himself of this, but to no avail. He straightened his sore back and held it up with one hand as he watched his breath float in the clear, cold mountain air. He didn't know what day of the week it was—he had lost track again. He and the other soldiers had been shoveling since the crack of dawn, and all he could think about was lunch.

He felt weak. His stomach was empty; constant hunger pain had become part of the daily routine. The last thing he had eaten was a cold potato the night before, along with some cold water he had fetched from a nearby creek. They had found some sugar beets, but they tasted horrible raw.

Gripping the spade with his dirty and calloused hands, he continued the monotonous task, relentlessly stomping down onto the beat-up tool and then throwing the dirt up onto the pile, again and again. As the trench got deeper and wider, the dirt piles got higher and higher. His muscles had grown over the last months, but his arms and legs were also sore from the daily labor, and he felt dirt everywhere. Under his fingernails was a pile of crud, and his face was dirty. His uniform clearly needed another wash. He couldn't remember the last time he washed it. He kept dreaming about a hot bath in his home, a bath he would soak in until the water got cold. Mutter would fire up the wood stove to get the bathwater to a boil, and one after the other, Mutter, Opa, Karl, or Hermann each would refill the tub for their turn until all the hot water would be gone. The next person in line for a soak would have to add the wood logs to the fire and wait another thirty minutes before being able to take a hot bath. They would have to keep feeding the wood stove to heat the bathwater until everyone had bathed.

Karl was still daydreaming, standing knee-deep in the ravine he had helped dig, when out of the side of his eye he caught a movement. He looked over and recognized someone running in the far distance down the grassy knoll toward them, screaming. Karl strained his ears to hear.

The screaming was muffled, the runner too far away for Karl to make out who it was and what he was saying. He stopped shoveling, with one last hard step on the spade to stand it up, and quickly moved toward the runner. Squinting against the morning sun, Karl strained his eyes until he finally recognized his comrade Anton closing the distance, screaming.

Finally, Karl could also make out the words:

"Der Krieg ist vorbei!"

He was sure he heard wrong. But Anton kept running toward them and repeating:

"Der Krieg ist vorbei! The war is over! The war is over!"

Karl couldn't comprehend it. Goosebumps prickled his skin, and suddenly the wind felt chillier than before. For a second, he almost felt paralyzed. His thoughts were somersaulting. Others with their dirty faces and dirty clothes now crawled out of their ditches as if in slow motion. None of them could believe what they were hearing. All gaped eagerly at Anton.

Karl broke into a run, sprinting toward Anton. He needed to hear it again.

Anton was waving his hands, screaming *"Der Krieg is vorbei!"* over and over as he barreled toward his fellow soldiers. He stumbled over his own feet on the dried cold dirt and tumbled to the ground.

Karl caught up to Anton as the boy tried to hoist himself up on his knees, hardly able to catch his breath. He must have been running for a while, and without much to eat in the past months, that kind of physical exertion took a major toll on the body. Karl grabbed Anton by his shoulders, propped him up with both hands, and looked hard into his eyes. "How do you know?" he demanded.

Anton stared through Karl. "Hitler killed himself!" he gasped. "I heard it—the war is over!"

Anton's chest was heaving, and he was breathing hard with each word. Excitement covered his muddy face, the smile lines around his hollowed eyes crinkling. "Can you believe it?! The war is over." His crooked teeth were widely exposed against his dirty face.

"Hitler killed himself? Who told you?" Karl barraged him with questions as he continued to prop his exhausted comrade up by his shoulders.

Anton's smile faltered a little, as if he were a bit annoyed at Karl for doubting him. "Feldwebel Bertrandt told me."

His breathing began to slow down, and he turned around to point at the Feldwebel, who now appeared in the distance, staggering down the hill as fast as his stubby, forty-year-old body would let him. Anton and the Feldwebel had been on a scouting mission to see how far the enemy fire was. They knew it was coming closer because they could see the fire at night. But during the scout, they had run into German soldiers who had heard the glorious news on their hand-held transmitters and receivers.

The group of trench soldiers now surrounded Karl and Anton, all eager to hear the latest information.

"What?"

"Hitler killed himself?"

Nobody seemed to really grasp what they were hearing. Hitler, so indestructible, killed himself? He had never given anyone the satisfaction of allowing them to kill him.

No, he had to kill himself and take away that privilege from anyone. His last hurrah, Karl mused bitterly.

After all this time, the war was finally over. After all their family hardships, being ripped from out of their mother's arms, Hermann being taken… Had Ferdinand really taken him back home? His missing Uncle Joseph!

Every soldier here had a similar story of missing brothers, fathers, cousins or uncles, most missing in action.

"*Nooooo!!!???*"

Schütze Milz cried out suddenly in fear of what would happen to him now that Hitler was dead and the country was in ruins, and his cry echoed in the cold mountain air.

The questions were flying.

"What does it mean?"

"Can we go home?"

 "How do we get home?"

 "Who will take us home?"

"Will the Russians take over?"

"The French? The Americans?"

 "Will we become prisoners?"

Nobody had any answers.

"They will kill us!"

"If the Russians reach us, they will kill us!" confirmed Anton. "I have heard they have orders not to take any prisoners."

"Anyone else can take us as prisoners—the Americans, the French, the English. But not the Russians," responded another soldier.

The uncertainty swiftly turned into panic.

Bach and Walter made a pact with each other right there to never surrender to the Russians.

"I would rather kill myself than have the Russians capture me!" They had all heard the horror stories of the Russian soldiers' brutalities: soldiers being killed on the spot, torture, stories of burning houses, rape of grandmothers and even children.

Some of the young trench diggers were visibly shaking, rubbing their arms, and teeth chattering, partially due to the cold air but mostly as a reaction to the news. None of them were really soldiers—they were kids, who had hardly fought in battle. They had only dug trenches.

But would the Russians believe them? Would the Americans care? Some of the boys were pacing back and forth, looking down and trying to find a solution, some looking at Karl for answers.

Karl motioned for everyone to slow down. He saw that even Hans's face had lost all its color.

Then Feldwebel Bertrandt finally got to the group. Everyone turned to him expectantly.

"Hitler is dead! We must surrender to the Russians," he announced, resigned. "They are about five kilometers that way." The soldiers followed with their eyes to where he pointed behind him.

"If we surrender, they will have to treat us as prisoners of war."

"I am not waiting around to be tortured by them," Bach exclaimed, panicked. He took off running west as fast as he could. Walter and some of the other soldiers immediately darted after him.

For a split-second, Karl thought about joining them as well. But he quickly changed his mind—he didn't want to be a deserter, and there was really no place to hide anyway. The Allies would catch up with them one way or another. No one knew what they could expect further inland.

Karl was still watching the soldiers dart away toward the west when he heard a scream: "No! Don't!" He wheeled around to see Feldwebel Bertrand leaping at Milz, who had snatched Bertrand's Mauser HSc handgun and now held it against his own temple.

"I'll never surrender!" Milz cried. The gunshot echoed through the gloomy mountainside.

"No!" Karl tried to stop the suicide, but Milz had already pulled the trigger. Karl, Bertrand and Anton tried to catch his fall, Anton holding the dead boy up in his arms. Blood was streaming down the right side of his face, leaking onto Anton's uniform.

"Schütze Milz, no, no, no," Anton whimpered, trying to hug the limp body. Milz had always been there for everyone, and they had become close the last few months here together. A few times, when Karl complained of hunger, Milz had even shared his potatoes with Karl, ignoring his own need for food.

Another shot echoed in the quiet cold air, and then another. They couldn't keep up with the mayhem that had broken out. Gefreiter Schenk shot himself. Milz and Schenk were close friends, and Karl and Hans had also grown close with both of them.

Another shot fired—Martin had shot himself—and it was followed by another shot.

More shots echoed through the mountain air as Feldwebel Bertrandt fired his rifle into the air, screaming, "Stop it! I order you all to stop it!"

Frantically, he tried to control the pandemonium that had broken out as the young soldiers feared they would become prisoners of war and be tortured.

"Put down your weapons! We have to surrender!"

"But why can't we try to defend ourselves? We have machine guns!" Albert cried desperately.

"We are outnumbered by the thousands—there is no use. It would be suicide trying to defend yourself here. You will only get us all killed. Now put down your weapons!"

Impatience was rising in the Feldwebel's voice. "Collect them here in a pile, so the Russians can see them openly."

Feldwebel Bertrandt put his own weapons down onto the ground, and Karl and Hans followed. Then one after the other, the soldiers hoisted the weapons off their shoulders and piled them on top of the others in the grassy field.

"The Russians will want the older SS," Feldwebel Bertrandt continued in an attempt to appease the younger soldiers.

Albert came to Feldwebel Bertrandt's support addressing the panicked group. "You all are mostly too young. They will leave you alone." He looked down solemnly as he spoke, because he knew what that meant for him.

Karl chimed in. "Yes, we had nothing to do with this. We were forced into this. I don't consider myself SS and never have."

There. He had said it. For the first time he had spoken publicly about what he had felt all along. No, he was not an SS. No, he did not believe, and had never believed, in the Nazi ideology.

Bertrandt and Albert just looked at Karl, not surprised. At this point, nobody cared enough to respond.

The Allied soldiers by then knew that SS could be identified by their blood type tattoo. But the Russians wouldn't care how willingly they joined the SS or how they got the tattoo. And given the language barrier, they wouldn't be able to communicate with each other.

Nobody spoke Russian, and, worse still, nobody would even take the time to listen to this explanation.

An older SS, *Unterscharführer* Schmidt, approached Karl with a razor blade between his beefy fingers.

What does he want? Karl wondered. Schmidt's demeanor had always made him feel uncomfortable; there was something odd about him that Karl couldn't figure out. Leaning in uncomfortably close against Karl's chest, Schmidt now stuck the razor blade in Karl's hand and half-whispered the order, "Here, cut it out," as he lifted up his arm, rolling up his sleeves and nodding at his SS blood-type tattoo on his underarm.

"What?" Karl asked in disbelief.

"Cut out the tattoo! They are going to kill me if they see it," Schmidt begged.

"But they will see the fresh wound right there. They can easily figure this out." Karl countered.

"I can tell them I got in an accident. I can make something up!" Schmidt was desperate, even though the request sounded utterly ridiculous to Karl. Anyone could figure out the source of that wound.

"Just cut it out!" Schmidt gritted his teeth, pleading.

"The tattoo is really deep; I will have to cut out a lot."

"Just cut it!" Schmidt held the blade close to Karl's throat, trying to intimidate him.

Karl grabbed it from Schmidt, and frustrated, started to puncture the *Unterscharführer*'s skin covering the flabby underarm. Blood began to pour out immediately. The tattoo was very deep—four or five millimeters deep.

Karl finally had to stop, turning away disgusted, with his hand covering his face. "I can't do this."

Schmidt impatiently ripped the razor blade back from Karl, tearing the skin on his thumb.

"Ouch!" Karl licked the drops of blood off his injured thumb.

Schmidt kept cutting at his own tattoo as he bit his lips and let out a continuous growl to suppress the pain. The tattoo was much deeper than he had expected. There was no way he could cut it all out, without leaving a deep gash, but Schmidt kept cutting.

Before Karl could run to try to get some cloth to wrap around the SS *Unterscharführer*'s arm, they were startled by the noise of a squeaky motor.

"Russians!"

The soldiers turned to see the Russian tanks in the distance, rolling down the same grassy knoll that Anton had just come from. The tanks easily rolled up and down through the trenches they had dug. Seven months of digging in vain! Nothing would stop those monstrosities.

"All, get ready to surrender," ordered Feldwebel Bertrandt calmly. "Put your hands up, everyone! Show them you are giving up! Otherwise, they will shoot you."

Feldwebel Bertrandt had wrapped a white cloth around the end of his machine gun as a sign of surrender, holding it up with one hand, his other hand also high up in the air as he stepped bravely forward in the direction of the convoy that was heading toward them.

The boys lined up side-by-side behind him with their hands up, anxiously awaiting their fate.

The three tanks squealed toward them. At least fifty soldiers marched on either side of each tank, their guns trained on Feldwebel Bertrandt and the young troops.

The tanks came to a stop in front of the ridiculously young, dirty, and skinny German soldiers, each of whom held their hands high in surrender. What must the Russians have been thinking, fighting a war with kids? Some of them probably had sons the same age, waiting at home for them to return.

Multiple Russian soldiers stepped forward with guns drawn. They stared at the group of child soldiers, mixed in with the set of young adults.

The front three Russians exchanged a few words. Then one of them took another step forward, and in broken German and gestures ordered the German soldiers to take off their shirts.

"SS here!" he ordered, pointing to his right with his rifle, and then to his left. "Non-SS here!"

Everyone moved to his right. They all bore the SS tattoo. They had all, pretty much, come together from being tattooed back in the Nürnberger headquarters. None of the soldiers here were direct *Wehrmacht* or non-SS, at least not based on their marking.

The young group of soldiers hesitated; they didn't want to be considered SS just because of the tattoo. They had had no part in the extreme brutality throughout the war that the SS was known for. They all at the same time unbuttoned their worn out shirts and quickly pulled off their sleeve, lifting up their arms to reveal their SS tattoos.

The Russian soldier looked astonished when he realized all of them bore the SS tattoo. He exchanged a few words with the soldiers behind him, then moved closer and started to tap each "trench-digger" on his shoulder, now hand-sorting them by age. Anyone who looked eighteen or over he tapped and ordered them to the left, and anyone who looked under eighteen he sent over to the right. He ordered everyone around with his rifle.

Hans was sent to the left with the older group.

Karl was sent to the right.

"No!" Karl tried to protest. But he was quickly silenced when the Russian soldier pointed his rifle at Karl's face. Karl wanted to follow his brother to the left, but with the rifle pointed at him, he did not dare disobey. With his hands up, he slowly walked over to the right.

Hans had always looked much older. He was tall for his age and broad-shouldered, and it would be difficult for him to pass for younger than eighteen. He had also sprouted a blonde mustache since he had arrived here, while Karl kept the few hairs that were growing on his face clean-shaven. The mustache made Hans look even older.

Why couldn't he have shaved that thing off? Karl was desperate, though not certain shaving would have even made a difference.

He could not believe what had just happened. Karl and Hans kept looking over at each other, from their two separate lines, one more worried about the other.

After less than thirty minutes, when all were sorted out, there were two hundred and thirty young soldiers lined up on the right and the forty older SS soldiers on the left. The rest had either fled or shot themselves.

"*Marsch*!" The Russian ordered the older group on the left to march back east, towards where they had come from. Two tanks, along with their assigned soldiers, turned around and led the way for this eastern convoy.

Karl still couldn't believe that Hans had been ordered to march with the older group. He watched as his brother marched away, a few rows behind Albert and the *Oberfeldwebel* Bertrandt. Karl felt the most helpless he had ever felt. There was nothing he could do at this point. His brother didn't belong with them, but he now had to watch them take him away together with Albert, the SS fanatic. Hans was the polar opposite of Albert—he had believed in this war as little as Karl had.

The Russian soldiers ordered the youngsters on the right to march inland toward Linz. The remaining tank headed west with them, leading the young prisoners of war. What would they be doing in Linz? What would Hans and the others be doing in the east?

The agony for Karl seeing his big brother march away with the rest of the older SS soldiers and those noisy tanks heading toward the east—the opposite direction he was going—almost brought him to his knees. He felt weak and nauseous. Karl held back tears of fear, frustration, and helplessness.

But it wouldn't do Hans any good if Karl passed out right there. He forced himself to get back in control, breathing deeply and letting the cold mountain air fill his lungs. He was only glad that Mutter was not witnessing this right now—she might not have survived this. Karl kept turning to look back east as he marched inland with the rest of the young soldiers, but the Russian guard directly next to Karl scuffed him in the shoulder with the butt of his rifle, motioning for him to march forward.

In the split second that Karl turned around, trying to look back for his brother, he was certain that he saw Hans turn around, too. They were already too far in the distance to really make out a face exactly. *Where were they taking him? Why did they separate them from the rest?*

The echo of a salvo of shots fired in the distance startled Karl out of his deep thoughts. Karl and the other soldiers instantly whirled around to frantically look in the direction of the fire. They could see a bunch of men lying on the ground in the distance there, executed by the Russian soldiers. Not all SS were shot, which was clear by the ones still standing in their grey SS uniform, but Karl still held his breath.

"Oh, my God!" was all he could say. They killed Hans! Shock and intense panic overcame him. He tried to run back east, but a Russian soldier pointed the rifle directly at his torso.

"стоп!" he ordered Karl, cold dark-brown eyes staring him down. Karl froze. He jerked his hands up and stared back. The rest of his group kept marching on, marching around Karl. Didn't anyone else care about these dead soldiers? Was Karl the only one with a relative in the other group? Had they all become so numb inside over these past months?

"Mein bruder!" Karl tried desperately to explain to the soldier, pointing with his face in the direction of the shots, still holding his hands up while choking back more tears. Complete panic had overcome him, and it took all of his self-control to not run toward the other group.

But it was clear the Russian either didn't understand Karl or didn't care. He didn't budge, his rifle still pointed at Karl.

"брат!" Alois, who had been further back, came up next to Karl and stopped to try and communicate with the Russian soldier. "брат!" Alois kept repeating the word, trying to get the Russian to understand, not knowing whether he would.

The Russian soldier looked again at Karl as if finally recognizing what Alois was saying. He also turned around for a split second to look in the direction of the distant older SS group. With the twenty or so soldiers now lying dead, the rest of that group had continued to march on toward the east, armed Russian soldiers on each side.

Why weren't all the SS killed? Did they pick the oldest? Had one of them tried to flee? What would happen to the rest?

Karl pleaded, *"Mein bruder, mein bruder,"* still pointing with his face in the direction of the dead bodies, with his hands barely up, bent at the elbow.

The Russian soldier turned back and motioned with his rifle again, directing Karl and Alois to turn around and catch up to the rest of the group, which was marching down the hill in the direction of Linz. They had no other choice but to turn around with the rifle pointed at them. They ran to catch up with the group.

Karl swallowed hard to hold in the tears. He and Alois reached the tail-end of the group. For every five rows of German soldiers five deep, there was a Russian soldier with a machine gun on each side. The young SS soldiers didn't stand any chance unarmed; to avoid being shot, they had no choice but to march along.

"It will be OK, they probably didn't get Hans," Alois whispered to Karl, trying to console him while marching, both looking straight ahead. Karl's agonized tears streamed down his red cheeks, each tear carving another path down his dirty face.

"I think I saw him walk away with the leftover group." Alois' well-meaning attempts to appease him didn't register with Karl. His mind was racing as he kept in step with Alois, marching on auto pilot. From his Hitler Youth days, had Karl learned to march while his mind was somewhere else.

How can I get back there and see who they shot? Will I ever see Hans again? Even if they killed him, I want to see him. I need to be sure. They can't just leave him lying there. What if he is just injured and needs help and is in terrible pain? Maybe they didn't kill him at all, because he is one of the youngest?

"Karl!" Alois hissed at Karl, realizing that he was not paying attention at all.

Back to the present for a moment, Karl looked straight ahead but whispered the impatient response, "What?" His steps did not falter. After a while, he murmured to Alois so the guards near them couldn't hear them, "The Russians will kill us, too. I am not sure where they are taking us, but they will kill us the same way they killed the others. We need to get away as soon as we can!" He was already forging his plan.

"What do you mean? How?" whispered Alois, terrified and nervously excited at the same time. Karl didn't respond, just stared straight ahead, and they all kept marching along the field toward Linz.

Their path led mostly downhill. A few kilometers down the country road they finally passed the faded yellow sign with black letters reading "Welcome to Plesching".

They saw smoke in the distance—a smoldering farm.

"Russians!" Karl was sure, and he wondered for a split-second what exactly happened here. But his worry for his brother again took over. Plesching was a quaint village on the outskirts of Linz, surrounded by the Alps. The houses sprinkled throughout the area were decorated with different shades of brown timber. Smoke slithered out of a few chimneys, but other than that the village looked deserted.

The church bells rang violently, warning the villagers that a large group of Russian soldiers was approaching, though nobody could have missed the noise of the loud squeaking tanks leading the soldiers heading towards them.

The group marched along the village's main road as it wound uphill. It was getting hard to keep up. The captured soldiers were cold, hungry and weak. *Where are they taking us?* Karl thought through the cadence. *Maybe to some sort of Russian makeshift internment camp?*

"Where do you think they are they taking us?" Karl heard himself asking out loud to Alois, who was still next to him.

No response. Alois just shrugged his shoulders. He would only be guessing, anyway.

Karl realized it was a rhetorical question. No one around him knew the answer, and the Russians certainly wouldn't tell him. Everyone was just marching along, entrenched in their own scared and worried thoughts, each just as exhausted and hungry as the next.

The paved village road was covered in patches of dried cow dung—leftovers from herding the cows to the pastures. Then the road wound left and narrowed, old houses framing either side of the road. For just a moment, the guards on each side of the soldiers were a few rows ahead of them.

"Run!" Karl hissed to Alois, and without much thought, Karl darted behind the house to his left. Alois reflexively followed. Not daring to looking back, they kept running, zig-zagging as if being chased by an army, expecting to be shot at any second, sprinting past house after house, running through shrubberies, a couple times jumping over fences. Running for their lives.

Completely out of breath, they arrived at the end of the tiny village. They heard a dog's angry bark in the distance. The houses had given them protection from sight, but now they would have to run across an open field lined by woods. While still running, Karl for the first time turned around to see if anyone was chasing them. There was no one.

He and Alois sprinted across the open field toward the thick underwood and trees at the end of the field that would give them much-needed coverage. They ran as if running the greatest race of their life.

When they were finally shielded behind trees, Karl stopped for a moment. Heaving and looking back again, he was surprised. "Did they not notice?" He could barely get the question out, he was breathing so hard. His lungs felt like they were burning.

"I don't know!" Alois was panicky and just as out of breath.

Karl had expected to be chased and to be shot at. But he knew they were not yet in the clear and they needed to get away. Laying down on the moss-covered ground, they looked back to where they had come from, scanning the open field through the trees, their chests still moving up and down.

"I don't trust it. It's too quiet. Where should we go?" Alois asked nervously.

"*Shhhh!* Let's just wait here for a bit. Wait and see if they come for us." Karl whispered.

They both cowered there quietly for a few more minutes, frantically watching and listening for any movement.

Karl whispered again without taking his eyes off the field. "Let's see if we can find a farmer who can hide us. The Russians will start looking for us. They will notice we are missing. If they haven't already. But first, we need to go back to the field and see if they killed…" Karl's voice trailed off. He swallowed hard. "Let's see who they killed."

Alois didn't respond. They sat up for a few minutes and continued to scour the direction they had come from. There was no movement at all, just empty fields with a few cows whose mooing could be heard. There was a light wind. The dog was still barking in the distance. Nobody seemed to be after them.

"I don't trust the silence," Karl said and jumped up again. "Let's go!" Before Alois could respond, Karl took the uphill path that would lead them back to the spot where they had been captured.

"Be careful," Alois hissed. "What if they expect us there? Can't we just hide here for a few hours?"

"No, and why would they?" Karl started sprinting again. He needed to find out whether his brother lay dying in that field; or worse, if he was already dead. Nothing was going stop him. Alois followed suit. The wind was howling more eerily than before when they finally got back to the open field where they had been captured just a little over an hour ago. The land here was elevated, and it was definitely colder than in the village. There was nothing here but dried field and a few flowers dotted throughout the grass. They saw the bodies lying in the distance, where they witnessed them being shot earlier, and Karl sped up. Alois was right behind him. The wind was blowing hard against them, as if to hold them back.

As they got closer, Karl slowed down to hold up his sleeve across his mouth and almost covered his eyes. He was afraid of what he was going to see. Alois walked hesitatingly next to him.

Before they got there, Alois had reminded Karl, "I don't think Hans is here. I am sure I saw him marching away with the rest. I recognized his broad-shouldered walk!" Karl wanted to agree with Alois. His gut feeling said that Alois might be right—he also thought for a split second that he saw Hans walk away with the rest—but he needed to be one hundred percent sure.

The sight of all the dead and bloodied bodies in front of them was vastly disturbing and frightening, and it would remain imprinted in Karl's memory forever.

Finally standing in front of the fallen bodies, they immediately recognized Feldwebel Bertrand's body lying there with eyes open, blood dried to the side of his mouth and neck. Anton's dead body was lying right next to Bertrand. No one moved; not a single sound besides the brisk wind and a few crows in the distance could be heard.

One soldier lay face down. Karl slowly walked toward him and got down on his knees to turn him over: It was Albert.

He looked peaceful; the stern look he had maintained since becoming an SS was wiped away. Albert had said the Russians would move forward only over his dead body—what a self-fulfilling prophecy! Though Karl didn't rejoice that Albert had died this way. If anything he would have wanted for Albert to have to pay in the court of law, not be killed by Russians. Deep sympathy for his former playmate overcame him. Karl remembered the few good times he had with Albert before he grew into this insane SS fanatic. The Nazi's had brainwashed him.

He didn't want to spend too much more time thinking about how sad it was for his former neighbor to have turned out like that. What would have happened to Albert if it wasn't for this war? Would Albert have gone on to learn a trade like his father, who had been a fine butcher until he too had become an SS fanatic? Wasted lives. It was a wasted war.

Karl took a step back over and leaned down to close Feldwebel Bertrandt's eyes. The Feldwebel had been a respectable person. Though he only did what he was told, he had treated everyone with as much dignity as he had in him.

"Let's feel everyone's pulse," Alois suggested, though they knew all were dead. He and Karl quickly grabbed the wrists of one soldier after another to check for life.

No pulse could be felt on any of them.

Karl felt relieved, and then instantly guilty at that sense of relief. But his brother was not one of the dead! Karl started feeling hopeful.

Maybe Hans could also escape? He looked east, wondering how close Hans and his group was.

As if reading his mind, Alois responded, "No, we can't go after them."

"I know," Karl responded, resigned. "We are outnumbered."

He looked back at the executed soldiers. "We need to bury them!" he decided.

"No, we need to get out of here! Look, everyone can see us kilometers away. We need to hide!" Alois was frantic.

Karl looked around. There was still nobody in sight; only empty space, with the beautiful Alps lining the background. But the scenic view didn't register in Karl's mind.

"Let's just move them into the trench over there and put dirt over them. They deserve to be buried. We can't leave them here like this," he insisted.

"The people from the village will eventually find and bury them!" Alois pleaded and attempted to yank Karl away so they could get going.

Karl ignored Alois' protest. "We don't even know when that will be."

Rolling up his sleeves, he bent down and grabbed Feldwebel Bertrandt's corpse by his boots, and started dragging it toward the freshly dug trench nearby.

Karl thought of the irony. *None of these dead soldiers imagined this morning when they were digging this trench that they were actually digging their grave.*

Karl sighed heavily. Exhausted, he used all the strength his young, malnourished body could provide to do the arduous work. Once finished with Feldwebel Bertrandt's body, he trekked back for the next dead soldier. Reluctantly, Alois grabbed Anton's body by the boots and did the same. They arranged all the dead soldiers next to each other in the trench, and once the last soldier was lined up, they start shoveling dirt over them.

"Mmmmmmmmmmmmm."

"What was that?"

"Moaning?"

Stunned, they both stopped immediately. Alois dropped his spade. They heard it again. "Mmmmmmmmmmm."

"Over there, it's coming from over there!" Karl pointed in the direction of the noise.

"It's Anton. The moan is coming from Anton!" Alois screamed frantically.

They ran back over to Anton and bent down to inspect him closely. Anton's left pant pocket was soaked in blood. Karl ripped off his own jacket, shirt and undershirt and pressed the undershirt against the wound. He didn't feel the cold air.

Anton moaned louder in a delirium, clearly in immense pain.

"Mein Gott!" said Karl. "He is still alive! We need to get him help. Let's take him to one of the farms we passed on the way here! Let's see if they can help."

Alois rolled his eyes. How could they do this without the Russians catching up with them? They needed to get themselves into safety first.

"We have to try!" Karl insisted.

Before they left, Karl quickly took the largest branch he could find and dug it into the half-finished grave to serve as a marker. It was more important to take Anton back to see if someone in the village could help than it was to finish this grave.

They both stood silently over the dead for a few seconds, quietly folding their hands for a quick prayer, then hurriedly crossed themselves and switched their focus back to Anton.

"Someone can give them a more deserving burial later on," Karl said, determined to make sure the villagers would find the grave. "We'll tell the next person we see in the village about this."

Karl scooped up Anton under both arms. His knees nearly buckled under the weight.

Anton kept moaning, barely conscious.

"Anton! It's Karl and Alois. We are here to get you some help!" Karl tried to comfort Anton, though he couldn't be sure that Anton heard him.

Karl turned to Alois. "We will take turns. I'll carry him for a while, then you."

Alois still tried to protest. "We could leave Anton here to get help. Then send someone come back here to get him!"

"How do you know we'll find anyone willing to help? If this was your brother or my brother, Hans, would you still say that? We have an obligation to take him and try to save him now!" Karl's mind was made up.

By then the sun had moved west. It was way past lunch time, and their stomachs were really feeling the emptiness.

"I am starving and parched!" Karl complained as he continued walking with the heavy load of Anton, who was getting heavier with each step. "*Mensch*, he is heavy!"

"When we ran here, did you see that farmhouse off to the left all by itself, with the smoking chimney?"

"Yes, and I also saw the one that was still smoldering. Did you see that one?" Alois was more than irritated that Karl seemed to be ignoring the fact that the Russians were nearby.

Yes, Karl recalled seeing that burned down farmhouse, too. But right now his focus was on the other farmhouse. It was surrounded by more land than the rest of them, plus the smoking chimney indicated someone had to be home.

He did have his concerns, though. *How far are the Russians from that farm? Why was one farm burned down but not the other?*

They didn't know whether anyone would even be home and would let them come inside. What if they shot at them instead?

Regardless, Karl and Alois both realized going there was their only option. Anton needed immediate help, and they needed to get out of these uniforms.

Karl and Alois switched schlepping Anton. The hike back to the farmhouse was exhausting, and a couple of times they nearly gave up, wanting to just put Anton down and leave him lying there. But step by step they kept at it, spurring each other on when either one was ready to quit. Sometimes, they carried him together, other times alone. Ten minutes at a time was the maximum each could handle. They counted the seconds out loud for each other—"one, two, three"—and it kept their mind off the strenuous task until they switched again.

Anton's moaning slowed, and they worried he wouldn't make it. It took them almost twice as long to get back to where they earlier passed the farmhouse. When they finally arrived at the farmhouse, Karl ran ahead and took the cement steps leading to the white front door in twos, banging at the door with both fists.

No answer.

He was certain someone had to be home. He could see the white smoke still slithering out of the chimney and the cows grazing in the grass behind the house.

Karl knocked again, louder this time, and waited another few minutes. Finally, the door squeaked open just a crack.

A middle-aged woman in a flowered apron peeked through the opened small space. Her kind brown eyes studied Karl, but then she saw Alois with bloodied Anton in his arms standing at the bottom of the stairs, and she quickly swung the door wide open.

"*Oh! Mein Gott,* what is going on?" She threw her hand in front of her lips at the sight and immediately rushed down the steps to help Alois carry Anton. "What happened? Hurry! Come inside! *Schnell, schnell!*"

Karl stepped back down, too, to help Alois get Anton up the steps, and the woman quickly rushed the boys inside.

They stepped into the warm, cozy home. The smell of freshly-baked bread lingered in the air. The living room they were standing in was connected to a dining room. An old, worn-out, green upholstered couch and a brown table covered by a flowered tablecloth, surrounded by a wooden bench, decorated the room.

On the other end of this large room was the kitchen, and nestled in a corner of the kitchen was a rustic, black iron wood stove with a tea kettle sitting on top of it, whistling the steam out of it. Lining the white kitchen wall were scratched cupboards.

The woman sped over to move the whistling tea kettle, silencing it. Then she turned around and said, "I will get a blanket for him and some cloths." She rushed out and quickly returned with a blanket. She hurriedly spread it on the couch and set the cloths on it, directing the boys while pointing to the couch: "Put him on here, carefully!" Alois and Karl worked together to gently lower Anton down.

"Let's see what we can do here." Sitting down on the couch next to Anton and leaning into him, she unbuttoned his uniform jacket. His left side was covered in crusted blood. The undershirt Karl had used to stop the bleeding was blood-soaked.

With the help of the boys, she removed the pants and inspected the wound. The bleeding seemed to have stopped.

"I'll use boiled water with some salt in it and at least try to clean out the wound. I am not a nurse, but I know the wound should be cleaned," she mumbled nervously as she headed for the kitchen, the cloths in her hand. She poured water from the teakettle into a bowl, mixed the water with some salt from the old cupboard, and dunked the cloths into it.

For a second Karl was impressed that these farmers still had salt. He hadn't tasted any in months.

The woman returned to Anton and dabbed the soaked cloth around the wound. Anton seemed to be in a deep sleep—he was not making any sounds. She felt for his pulse and could barely feel it. But he was still alive.

The two boys stood over her, watching her helplessly.

Suddenly the woman again jumped up and ran toward the back of the kitchen to open a door that led downstairs. "Wilhelm!" she screamed. *"Schnell,* Wilhelm, come upstairs!"

"What?" a deep grumpy sounding voice responded as they heard fast footsteps coming up from the barn. Within seconds, a tall, burly, middle-aged man with sandy hair walked through the door, dressed in blue overalls and a faded white undershirt.

"What is this?"

He stared at Karl and Alois standing by the couch with the half-undressed and blood-stained Anton lying on it. A shadow fell over his face *"Mein Gott,* who are they?" He looked at his wife accusingly, irritated and at the same time scared.

"Look at them! They are kids, and they need help!" she responded, trying to calm him.

Wilhelm turned to Karl and Alois and demanded, "What is going on? What happened to him?" motioning with his large beard-stubbled chin at Anton, lying on the coach. "Who are you?"

"Did you hear the war is over? Hitler killed himself," Alois jumped in.

"Yes, I heard on the radio!" Wilhelm responded, letting Alois sidetrack him for a split second. Then he squinted at them again. "But what happened to you all? Why are you here in my house? Have Russians followed you?" he asked.

Anxiously Wilhelm stepped over to one of the kitchen windows, slightly pushing aside the curtains, peering outside to see whether anyone had followed them. Then he moved over to the living room window and did the same.

"Nobody has followed us!" Karl said firmly, though he couldn't be sure himself. He felt a twinge of guilt about possibly endangering this couple. What if the Russians were still looking for them? He started talking as quickly as he could. Everything he had kept bottled up in his mind the last couple of months was pouring out.

He introduced himself and Alois, and explained all the details—how they were grabbed from their homes by the SS, how they were indoctrinated into the SS without any specific training, how they had spent the last months digging trenches up on the hill not far from there, and how he even spent a few days at the front. He went on to explain how just a few hours ago, they were captured by the Russians, and that they had shot Anton. Anton, along with the others, had been left for dead.

Karl babbled on about his brother, how he and Alois had just fled the Russians, and how—

Wilhelm stopped him. "You can't stay here!"

The boys look at him, scared.

"Wilhelm!" the wife tried to object.

But the farmer firmly shook his head.

"A neighbor farmer was shot and killed yesterday. Did you see that burned farmhouse just down the hill? It is still smoldering. That was his farmhouse. I heard Wassermann, the farmer, was shot on the spot. He had been hiding three German SS soldiers, and the Russians found them. They killed Wassermann and his family and burned his farm down. It is much too dangerous for my wife and me to hide you here! The Russians have been raping and murdering. They are animals. I don't think there is a female in town who hasn't been raped by them." He glanced at his wife, who was looking down. "Except Lisl, so far. She is one of the few. We want to keep it that way, and we want to stay alive!"

His wife jumped in, pleading, "Look at the boy," pointing toward Anton. "He is severely injured; he needs help. And these boys are starving! Give them one night. I'll give them something to eat. They can borrow some of Markus' clothes, and we will send them off first thing in the morning. Just give them one night's good rest and a good meal! Wouldn't you want someone to help Markus if he needed help now?"

Karl and Alois held their breath, eagerly anticipating Wilhelm's response. Karl wondered fleetingly who Markus was, but came to the conclusion he must be their son. Wilhelm stared at his wife as if his immediate reaction was to say no, but then he looked at Anton again as if he was just realizing the perilous condition the boy was in.

Sighing, defeated, Wilhelm agreed, "Alright, but one night only! You absolutely have to leave before daylight! Nobody can see you leave this farm! I hope no one saw you coming here."

Karl and Alois exhaled, relieved for the moment. This would give them one more night away from the Russians. They would figure something else out tomorrow. Maybe their captors had given up searching for them; or better yet, maybe they hadn't even noticed the boys were missing. But Karl knew that the Russian soldier who had stopped him from chasing after Hans would remember him. Their eyes had locked.

"I am Elisabeth Bauer," the woman said with a slight smile. "Just call me Lisl." She shook each boy's hand. "And this is my husband, Wilhelm." She smiled as she grabbed her husband's arm.

"Maybe we can get Doctor Weinsteiger to come, Wilhelm?" She looked at her husband pleadingly. Before he could respond, she explained to the boys, "Weinsteiger is retired, but he can help here more than any of us. He lives just a few farmhouses over. We can trust him."

Wilhelm reluctantly agreed and said he'd take his bike over to see if he could get Dr. Weinsteiger to come over immediately.

He again reminded the boys not to leave the house until it was either pitch dark or first thing in the morning, before sun-up. "It will be death for all of us if we are caught harboring soldiers."

The boys assured him they were not planning to go anywhere in daylight.

Wilhelm slammed the door shut as he left, and they could hear him lock it behind him. Then his heavy footsteps could be heard racing down the steps.

Lisl offered the boys slices of the big brown loaf of bread they had noticed sitting on the kitchen counter on an *Edelweiss*-flowered plate.

"Can I have some water first?" Karl was so relieved she would offer them something to eat.

"Oh, of course! You are thirsty. Get some glasses," she pointed in the direction of the old wooden kitchen cupboard. "Get water from the bucket over there; it's fresh from the well."

The two obliged and quickly gulped two glasses of water in a row. "I would like to get a slice of that bread, please," Alois asked politely.

"Of course, take it!" she offered.

Recently out of the oven, the bread was still warm and soft, and its scent continued to fill the air. They hadn't eaten fresh bread since they had been home. The young men devoured the bread to the last crumb.

"Some fresh milk is there too," Lisl offered. "I boiled it; the skin is still on top. Let me strain it." Lisl strained the milk into two mugs and handed them to the boys. "Here, it's still warm."

Freshly baked bread and warm milk. After what they had been living on, Karl was sure he had never eaten any food this good.

"And when you are finished with that, I have some alcoholic apple cider, if you want?"

"*Most*?" Karl and Alois' eyes widened. Yes, they would love some. Lisl poured them each a glass. It was a feast and more food and drink in one sitting than they both had consumed in over seven months.

In the background, they heard Anton's slight groans. He seemed to be coming to again. Maybe he didn't want to be left alone. Lisl walked over and touched Anton's arm lightly. "You will be alright," she said softly.

Karl and Alois watched her as they savored the warm milk. There was not much they could do for Anton except wait. Lisl was providing all the comfort they could garner at that point. Hopefully, Wilhelm would come back with that doctor soon.

Lisl left the kitchen through an opposite door that led upstairs, and a few moments later, she came back, her arms loaded with men's pants, shirts, and socks, and two pairs of shoes. She could barely balance it all in her arms.

"Here, see if these fit you. We need to get you out of these uniforms."

She set the clothes and shoes down on the wooden bench next to the dining room table. When one of the shoes dropped onto the wooden floor, Alois quickly jumped to pick it up for her.

The boys looked at her, then the clothes, inquisitively. And as if she could read their minds, she explained.

"These clothes belong to Markus, our son. He was sent to the Eastern Front in 1943. He used to write us letters, but we haven't received any from him in over a year." For a minute she looked up at the picture hanging on the wall of her son in his *Wehrmacht* uniform, as if by studying his picture she could get answers about his fate.

"See if his clothes can help you at least." She changed the subject.

"How old is Markus?" Alois asked, concerned.

"He turned twenty-four two months ago." Lisl looked down, but Karl could see the sadness that had overcome her face. "Another one of his birthdays we have missed."

Karl and Alois looked at each other, knowing that if one hadn't heard from their kin in such a long time, the chances of him coming back were slim.

"Change already!" she ordered them, forcing herself to snap out of the moment of sadness that had overcome her.

Quickly they stepped away into the back of the living room, turning away, and then tore off their uniforms, so happy to get rid of them. Then they rushed to put on the new clothes.

It was such a relief to once again be in civilian clothes.

Karl looked around to see if anyone was watching, but Lisl was looking the opposite direction to give them privacy. He sneaked the pocket knife out of his uniform pant pocket into his new civilian pants pocket. He had been lucky. The Russians had not bothered to check whether he had any weapons, regardless how small.

The clothes were a bit loose and baggy on Alois but fit Karl almost perfectly; while the shoes were a bit big on Alois, they were almost too tight for Karl. But the fit was close enough. Alois had to roll up the pant legs and sleeves twice each.

Lisl picked up their dirty uniform pants and jackets from the floor and carried the pile over to the wood stove to shove in the first pair of pants. "We have to burn all evidence," she said, winking at them, "one piece at a time. We should get the rest of the clothes off Anton, too. Once the doctor is here, we can work on that."

Not even twenty minutes had passed when Wilhelm unlocked the door and rushed inside, shutting it swiftly behind him. Was he being followed?

Karl watched as he carefully peeked behind each curtain again to make sure he wasn't. Then he excitedly, but in a hushed tone, proclaimed that Dr. Weinsteiger was on his way.

"I found him sweeping his barn. He will be right over." And looking at the boys, he ordered, "You boys need to go hide in the barn right now!" Wilhelm sternly pointed to the direction of the barn downstairs and adjacent to their house.

"Grab a few blankets for them, Lisl. They need to stay there throughout the night." Lisl stood from the wood stove and hurried off.

Wilhelm turned back to the boys. "Before sunlight, you both need to be out of here. We know Dr. Weinsteiger well, but nowadays you can't trust anyone completely. It's bad enough we will have to make up something about how we found this guy," Wilhelm nodded toward Anton, "but Dr. Weinsteiger doesn't need to be burdened knowing about you two."

Lisl came back with grey, rough-looking woolen blankets and handed one to each boy.

"Don't sleep near the barn entrance. Hide behind the haystacks as far back as possible," she advised them. She sounded worried. "And when you leave in the morning, make sure you stay away from Russian territory. You must run west for at least fifteen kilometers, through the forest, and always keep to the right. Then you'll come to a road. Walk up it a few kilometers, and you will see the railroad tracks. You will have to cross them, and then keep walking, and you'll be in American sovereign territory."

"One more thing," Wilhelm somberly interjected. "Together with our priest, we'll find that spot you've described where the dead soldiers are, and we'll make sure to give them a worthy burial."

That was one of the most comforting things Wilhelm could have told them. This farmer and his wife truly were good people. Their kindness made Karl and Alois eager to hide in the barn—they didn't want to get the couple into any trouble. Especially not after they had been treated so well by them.

"Now listen and do what Lisl said!" Wilhelm ordered. "Go as far back and up in the barn as you can!"

Lisl ran back to the kitchen and quickly returned with two warm potatoes for each boy.

"Here's a little bit more food for you two!" She smiled as she handed them the potatoes.

Karl put half of one in his mouth and bit down to hold it in place as he gathered up his blankets. With the blankets and the rest of the potatoes in their hands, the boys headed through the back kitchen door, down the stairs, and then through another door that led them into the barn attached to the farm.

"Do you think the Russians are still looking for these boys?" Lisl whispered to Wilhelm nervously.

"I have a feeling they are…"

In the barn, Karl and Alois walked across the squeaky wooden planks that covered the barn floor, passing spades, pitchforks, and ladders hanging on the side of the timber wall. They climbed over haystack after piled haystack as far back and as high as they could, as far away from the front barn entrance door as possible. When they finally were in the farthest and highest corner of the barn, Karl moved one of the haystacks in front of them. Their hideout was complete.

They tried to make themselves comfortable, though the hay was starting to make them itch. Karl spread out his blanket to lie on, and they used Alois' blanket to cover themselves. They quickly ate the rest of the potatoes, and completely exhausted, they both started to drift off.

"I wonder how Hans is doing," Karl asked before completely nodding off.

"I am sure he is fine," Alois muttered drowsily. "Let's go to sleep."

Within a few minutes, they slipped into a deep slumber. The unbelievable happenings of the day had left them exhausted.

****

"Where are they?"

Karl's eyes flashed open, ripped awake by Russian sounds. Both he and Alois were immediately wide awake, staring at each other in sheer fear. Early sunlight was already streaming inside the barn. They must have overslept, and the Russians were here looking for them!

Karl put his finger to his lips to motion to Alois to be quiet. He pulled the knife from his pocket. They tried to hold their breath. Neither dared to move.

It sounded like there were at least two Russian soldiers, if not three. The voices were coming closer—they were climbing toward them on the haystacks. The boys could hear pitchforks stabbing inside the haystack.

Crouching down as low as possible, Karl and Alois quietly scooted back until they felt the barn wall on their backs. There was no more room for them to move. Karl had his knife in his hand, ready, even though it was only a small pocket knife.

They could hear the Russians coming closer and closer, stabbing the haystacks over and over until they could actually see a pitchfork stabbing through the haystack in front of them. Karl's heart skipped a beat. They both held their breaths.

They heard one of the Russians say something to the other, standing right next to them, only three haystacks separating them. A few moments of silence followed. The boys still barely breathed.

A loud crash came from outside, as if something large had collapsed or dropped.

Silence followed. After a few seconds, Karl could hear the Russians speaking again, but now the voices seemed a bit further away. It sounded as if they had turned back. The pitchforks stabbing the haystacks had also stopped. The voices slowly grew fainter, moving farther and farther away.

Karl and Alois looked at each other. They sat there quietly, without a word, for what seemed like an eternity. Was anyone still there? They did not dare to move for a while, even though ten minutes had passed without any sounds.

Finally, they slowly peeked from behind the bales, climbing cautiously over the haystacks, keeping a sharp eye out for anyone left inside the barn. But the front barn door was wide open, and nobody was inside any longer. The Russians seemed to have given up and left.

"We have to go!" Karl whispered, and without waiting for a response, he scrambled the rest of the way over the pile of haystacks and down toward the barn front door; Alois followed close behind. They paused briefly to look out the small window high up on the side of the barn. The haystacks were piled so high that they only had to step on their tiptoes to see outside the window. The angle didn't allow them to see anyone directly under the window and not much to the sides of it, but they could only see fields and clear sky for miles straight ahead.

"I think they are gone."

When they got to the barn door, they carefully glanced around the door, looking left and right, to make sure the Russians were really gone.

"Look!" exclaimed Alois as he pointed to the south down the hill. Specks of three soldiers could be made out walking far in the distance. Karl and Alois ducked back inside.

"They are walking toward the village!" Karl whispered. "Let's go the opposite direction, back east, and then we'll follow the directions west through the woods, just how Frau Lisl described them!"

After waiting a bit longer inside the barn door, Karl and Alois confirmed one last time that the Russian soldiers had completely disappeared from sight. Then they darted out of the barn and ran up the hill, into the woods. Out of the corner of his eye, Karl could see the farmhouse's curtains move. He was sure Lisl and Wilhelm had been watching all that happened from their windows. How relieved they must have been to see everyone go away.

Karl felt incredibly guilty that they stayed into the morning light. How did they not wake up earlier? How could they have put the nice farmer and his wife into such danger? *It must have been the cider.* They should have never even drunk that one glass, though Lisl had meant well.

They were lucky the Russians didn't find them. It was so close, and if they had found them, they would have certainly shot them and the farmer and his wife on the spot. The barn and farmhouse would be burning right now. Karl would forever be thankful to Wilhelm, the farmer, and his wife, Lisl, who took them in for one night, and who gave them food and civilian clothes. He would always remember Lisl, especially, as the kindest woman Karl had met throughout all of the war.

They didn't know what would happen to Anton. Was the doctor able to help him? Maybe the couple had hidden Anton somewhere when the Russians showed up; or maybe the Russian soldiers had only looked for them in the barn.

The boys continued to run through the woods. The plan was to stay inside the deep forest as long as they could, always heading west. They wanted to get far away from the Eastern Front where the Russians were advancing. They were too far away from home to be walking out in the open—even in civilian clothes, they could be stopped by the Russians.

They felt somewhat safer deep in the woods. Surely the Russians wouldn't come this far in, and their tanks couldn't get through all those big pine trees. Karl and Alois remained on guard for foot soldiers who could eventually cross their paths, however.

Deep in the woods, they stopped to drink water from a creek and eat a few barely-ripe berries. They tasted some of the raw nettle they found, too; but it tasted even more bitter than they were used to. Karl didn't want to risk another night of diarrhea like the one at the front. His stomach had hurt so badly that night that he wasn't sure he would make it. Karl spit out the raw nettle, telling Alois his green apple story and the pain and bathroom consequences. Alois also spit the nettle back out. They both needed to stay healthy.

The boys kept moving along until they stumbled onto large clusters of blueberries. Everywhere they could see there were bushes of them. "My favorite berry!" Karl exclaimed as he quickly bent down to pick them by the handful and shove them into his mouth.

"Mmmmh!" Alois also voiced his approval as he started to chomp down on them as well. They were some of the sweetest blueberries they remembered ever eating. Their lips turned blue from them.

But after twenty minutes of eagerly feasting on them, Karl pushed to keep going. As much as he would have wanted to eat every berry in sight, they had to press on to get away from the Russian zone. They walked on.

They often took breaks, sitting on patches of moss wondering what their future would hold. Karl's shoes now were starting to pinch his toes, and he could feel the blisters starting to form on his heels. Karl and Alois spent most of that day in the woods. When they didn't stop to rest, they walked.

The directions Lisl had given them were simple to follow. After walking about fifteen kilometers west, the boys emerged from the forest's awning to walk down the road, following the directions Lisl had given them. When they thought they had walked long enough, they began looking for the railroad Lisl told them about. But there was still no railroad crossing in sight.

The sun was starting to set, and worry was beginning to creep in, when they finally stumbled upon the tracks. They crossed over with spirits renewed, and then a few kilometers after crossing the old tracks they re-entered the forest parallel to a dirt road.

Suddenly Karl stopped, holding up his hand for silence.

Trucks!

They immediately darted back inside the forest and crouched behind large pine trees to wait and see whether it was another Russian convoy.

And then Alois cried out, "Americans!" He had recognized the American flag.

"Americans!" Karl screamed. "Americans! Let's surrender!"

Karl pulled out his pocket knife and dug it into the moss at the spot where they were squatting. He would leave it there for good.

"Let's go!"

He jumped up with his hands raised high and ran up the dirt road, Alois right behind him. Karl glanced back at him and hissed, "Your hands!" and Alois quickly threw his hands up as well. They both walked straight toward the American convoy.

What a sight that must have been for the American GIs. These young boys—Karl only sixteen and Alois only a year older—blue-lipped and dressed in civilian clothes, holding their hands up high in surrender. The leading truck in the convoy slammed on the brakes, and the soldier walking next to it kept his rifle ready as he walked up to the boys. "Do you speak English?"

"Nein! Nein Englisch," was all Karl could respond with. He could not speak any English but understood enough of it to respond to the soldier's question.

The soldier hollered over his shoulder at another soldier further back in the convoy.

"Sergeant Fritz, come up here! I need you to translate." Quickly another soldier appeared from the group of soldiers who now surrounded the two young boys.

Sgt. Fritz, in perfect German, asked the boys, "Are you armed?"

"No," they responded in unison.

"Roll up your sleeves!" Sgt. Fritz knew to look for the SS tattoo— enough child and adult SS had surrendered to them. Both Karl and Alois rolled up their sleeves and revealed their SS tattoos.

Karl quickly told them the boys' story, and how they were fleeing the Russian soldiers.

"They are pilfering, killing, and burning farmer's houses down!"

Sgt. Fritz just nodded knowingly. "Yes, they are animals. But now, come with us."

Sgt. Fritz translated for his staff-sergeant that the boys were dragged into the SS against their will.

"Look at them!" he exclaimed, shaking his head. "They are kids!"

But the staff-sergeant was not as quick to sympathize. "That's what they all say," he replied. "But they are still SS! We'll have to take them to the SS camp."

That day, Karl and Alois became American prisoners of war.

Though they were somewhat relieved to be free of the Russians, they didn't know what would await them next.

Chapter 8

Camp

The American GIs brought the two boys to a POW camp—a set of barracks previously used by the German defense near Linz. The site had quickly been turned into a makeshift camp for the younger German POWs who were arriving daily. The barracks were also surrounded by a sea of temporary American Army military tents and some Red Cross tents.

After only a few days of being in American captivity, Karl counted one hundred young soldiers before he quit counting.

The German-speaking Sgt. Fritz had explained to Karl and Alois that they would have to follow orders and work for the American GIs. They each were asked for their personal information, such as their first and last name, any crafts or skills, and more. Karl, for the first time in a long time, mentioned his nearly-finished carpentry apprenticeship. The Americans didn't ask the boys about their addresses or their parents; for now, they were only POWs.

Then, without explanation, Alois and Karl were separated. Karl was given quarters in one end of the barracks, and Alois was situated on the other end of the camp. The Americans must have figured that each of them on their own would be less prone to scheming, Karl assumed. Though both boys were way too hungry and too far from home to do anything but what they were told. And after all, they had willfully surrendered to the Americans in fear of the Russians.

Karl was placed into a barracks room with a young SS named Max, who had surrendered to the American GIs a few days earlier. A few days later, Wilfried and Frederick were added.

The bunk beds filled quickly, and some of the captured had to sleep on the floor. Fights over beds would become common. Karl pleaded with the GIs to not add any additional POWs to their already crowded room. At this rate, they would kill each other over a bed.

Each of the captives had similar stories to tell: they were all teenagers, pulled into the war months ago. They were all tired and hungry because they also had been running from the Russians.

There was a common sense of relief that they had been "captured" by the Americans instead of the Russians. All of them had heard about the Russian atrocities. Captured SS soldiers were shot on the spot, or worse, slowly tortured to their deaths. Some had witnessed this cruelty with their own eyes.

It was not until much later that the young soldiers would learn that the German soldiers on the Russian front were equally atrocious, and much of this inhumane treatment was considered payback by the Russians.

The captured teenagers were all desperate to go home. Hitler was dead, the war in Germany was over—a war none of these young kids chose to fight—and they were eager to know the whereabouts of their loved ones. Karl listened to all of them telling similar stories after he had grown tired of telling his own. Wilfried kept talking about how much he missed his mom; Frederick really missed his younger brother; and everyone else wondered what had happened to their family.

How long would they be held in this makeshift American prison camp? How long would the Americans stay here? Would they take over the German government? The Americans sure were a far away from home.

Karl thought he would be fine with the Americans being in charge of Germany, though he didn't know what that would entail. America, in his mind, had always been a glamorous, faraway country to which many Germans had emigrated.

Karl still remembered the excitement of Opa and Mutter during the 1936 Olympics, though he was only eight years old at the time. They cheered on the black Olympian, Jesse Owens, who won the long jump gold medal against the German rival Carl Ludwig "Luz" Long. Hitler had wanted to show the world how the Aryan race would beat everyone in the Olympic Games, but Jesse Owens proved otherwise.

Then, much to Hitler's displeasure, Luz Long became friends with Jesse Owens. When the American won one of his four Olympic gold medals, Luz even ran a victory lap with him. Long's mother, Rudolph Hess—appointed Deputy Führer to Adolf Hitler—ordered Luz never to hug a *Neger* again.

When the war broke out, Luz was later sent to the front, where he was killed—many thought it was to punish him.

The German public adored Jesse Owens. And he was the epitome of an American to Karl—he expected most Americans to be athletic and impressive like Jesse.

In the American prison camp, twice a day the boys were fed stale bread and watery soup with some potatoes, but mostly unidentifiable chunks floating in it. It was hardly enough nourishment for growing boys; their youth was what helped them get through these starving days.

While the sun spread warmth during the day, at night the barrack walls were not thick enough to keep out the cold, five-degree Celsius air out. Even with the few scratchy blankets they were provided, they were always cold. The GIs were short on heating wood.

The German youngsters were allowed to walk around somewhat freely within the perimeter of the camp, but GIs were everywhere, and armed soldiers were guarding each of the four corners of the enclosed area, marked by a makeshift wire fence, with a tank on each corner and two tanks along each of the four sides surrounding the camp.

On his third day in captivity, Karl was starting to feel bored. During the past few days they had been there, they hadn't been doing much. They had to take out their own trash and keep their rooms clean, but other than that, one day after another had been a copy of the day before. Karl was getting the impression that the GIs were just trying to figure out what to do with all of these SS soldier boys.

That morning, though, Max was picked up by a Sergeant for an undetermined task. The sergeant had marched into their room before dawn and ordered for Max to get dressed and to come with him.

That had been the first time any of them were called to duty. Nobody in the quarters knew what exactly that was about, why only Max had been singled out. But then they heard the Sergeant say to Max "We need help from the strongest and most muscular boy in the quarters!"

Later that same morning, Karl roamed the grassy area near the food trucks, scavenging for leftover food. He found a few potato peels and carrot chunks in a large metal bucket used for collecting tossed food scraps and other trash. Carefully scanning the area to ensure that nobody was watching him, Karl bent down and grabbed the leftovers. He stuffed some of the food morsels into his pockets, and others straight into his mouth. It all tasted bitter, but he would do anything to get rid of those hunger pangs. And the scraps were surprisingly a nice change from the bland soup broth and stale bread the GIs were feeding him.

In the past few days, Karl had also been gathering nettle growing at the perimeter of the camp. He would uproot the plant, hide it in his pocket, and then clean off any dirt and secretly eat it when nobody was looking. It tasted less bitter than the nettles he and Alois had found in the woods, and became a new supplement to his daily diet, whenever he could find it.

Out of the corner of his eye, Karl noticed a black GI passing by. Karl had never met a *Neger* in person until he had arrived at the camp. He stopped his scavenging for a moment and nodded a greeting to him. The black soldier turned away, pretending not to notice, as Karl went back to digging through the trash for more scraps.

"Stop that!"

Before Karl could finish his scavenging, a pock-faced private, at most five years older than him, yanked him by his jacket collar away from the trash.

"Stop eating from the trash!" he repeated, slapping Karl's scraps out of his hand. Karl chewed the rest of the potato peel and swallowed it as fast as he could. Karl pleaded with his eyes with the young private, with a nametag that read "Miller", telling him he was just hungry. But Miller's piercing blue and determined eyes stared hard back at Karl.

"Stop that!" he repeated again in English. "You could get sick from that!"

Although Karl didn't speak any English, he could tell by the Private's tone that he vehemently disapproved of Karl's digging through the trash.

"Get away from the trash!" Miller ordered sternly, releasing Karl's collar and shoving him in the opposite direction of the scrap bucket. He waved his arm to chase Karl away as if to shoo away a stray dog. Karl adjusted his collar, tucked in his shoulders, put his hands in his pants pockets, and looked down as he headed back toward his barracks building. He arrived back at his hall frustrated, deep in thought, and still hungry.

"Tomorrow we are starting work!" Frederick announced to him, lying in his bunk chewing on a piece of nettle. He also had picked up the habit of eating the bitter weed.

Karl looked up, surprised. "What do you mean? What kind of work?"

"They were looking for laborers," Frederick was saying.

"Carpenters. And you told them you had been a carpenter apprentice, right? One of the sergeants was asking, and I told him you—"

Before he could finish, a sergeant stepped into the room—the same sergeant that Frederick must have been talking to. In broken German, he asked Karl, *"You are carpenter?"*

Karl looked at the sergeant inquisitively. "Yes, I took part in a carpenter apprenticeship for a few years."

That was more German than the sergeant could comprehend. He shook his head, repeating what he said before. "Slow down. You are carpenter?"

Karl shortened his response to make it easier to understand: *"Ja, ich bin ein Schreiner!"*

The sergeant's face lit up at the confirmation. "We need your help! We will come by to get you tomorrow."

Karl put the tips of his fingers together and moved them back and forth, to and from his mouth, to motion he was hungry. He pleaded with the sergeant, "I am too hungry. I can't work like this."

The sergeant surprisingly understood and responded with, "No worry, where you are going tomorrow there will be food." And with that, the sergeant left.

Karl was eager to find out where he was supposed to apply his carpentry skills, and more importantly where he finally would get more food. How he longed for the feeling of a full stomach after one of his Mutter's warm meals, and for the first time in a long time, he was looking forward to the next day.

The thought of the unfinished desk for the Major ran through his mind. *Did Mutter and Opa get it finished?* He sure hoped so. He hadn't thought about it for a while now, but he shuddered again just thinking about the multitude of possible consequences if the desk and chair weren't done to spec, and on time. The Major would take no excuses.

****

It was May 13, 1945, and it was sunny, though the air was crisp and cold. White clouds hung stark against the pale blue sky, the majestic grey mountains lining the horizon.

"To the gate, now!" ordered Sgt. Fritz in his deep thunderous voice as he used his entire body to gesture north to the gate, where a truck was sitting. Today was the start of a new work detail for Karl and a few others. What exactly they would be doing and where they would be working was not yet clear to them.

It had been another cold night in the American prison camp. Karl was the last one to climb out of his bunk. But he raced out the barracks door toward the opening in the wire fence as fast as his long young legs could take him. Max, Wilfried, and Frederick, along with a few other German POWs had already lined up there. The steam of their breaths could be seen blowing in the cold mountain air.

They were all waiting, heads down, with hands in their coat pockets, trying to use the small woolen space to keep at least their hands warm, since the rest of their bodies couldn't seem to warm up. The GIs had handed all of them scratchy woolen coats, some in better condition and better fitting than others. Karl was still wearing the clothes Lisl had given him underneath his "new" coat.

Wilfried and Frederick were looking down, moving the grey stone gravel and dirt back and forth with their feet as if it were a contest. The burly Max looked up when he heard Karl approach, squinting against the rising sun, and gave Karl a slight nod. Wilfried and Frederick never looked up, fiercely focused on the gravel game.

A truck was parked right next to one of the tanks that marked the camp's border. As its driver started the engine, the rattling motor disrupted the eerie silence of that fresh May morning. The smell of burning diesel filled the air.

Another sergeant, whom Karl hadn't seen before, stood next to Sgt. Fritz in front of the truck, holding his rifle over his shoulder. Karl squinted at the sergeant's name tag—"Rotz"—and he wondered whether Sgt. Rotz knew that his American name in German meant "snot". He was slightly amused; a reaction he was surprised to feel, as he hadn't felt it in a long time. He thought again of how relieved he was that the war was over and that he was with the Americans.

But then a pang of hunger rumbled through his gut. His stomach lining felt like it was getting ready to digest itself. Why couldn't the GIs give them more to eat? Karl knew they also had little food, and more food trucks were expected any day. But whenever the trucks got there, the GIs were the first ones to be fed, and the young POWs were left with the leftovers.

Sgt. Fritz's voice pulled Karl from his complaints, as the sergeant shouted out the last names of the young captives' one at a time for roll call:

"Schmidt!"

"*Hier!*" answered Max.

Fritz marked off Max's name.

"Elheusch!"

"*Hier!*" replied Karl.

Fritz checked off the rest of the names as each one responded with confirmation.

As the sergeant continued the roll-call, Karl pondered the German last names and their origins: Fritz, Rotz, and he had seen others. Certainly they all had German ancestors. *How long ago did they emigrate to the United States? Do their parents or grandparents still speak German? Do they still have distant relatives in Germany? What would it feel like for an American soldier with German ancestry to have to come back to the homeland of their ancestors and fight against them?*

Karl could only imagine the potential internal conflict this dilemma posed for them.

Fritz yelled in German: "We have the right guys here! And I have all your names, so don't think we are not tracking you."

Sgt. Rotz then stepped in and ordered the boys into the back of the truck. The young prisoners of war didn't need to understand English; they could read Rotz's body language. Moving his rifle butt back and forth, he got them to quickly climb in the back of that truck. "Hurry! *Auf, auf! Schnell, schnell!*"

Karl was not sure what the big hurry was, but he and the other boys jumped up into the truck and filed into the back. One by one they sat down on the cold floor of the cab and huddled close together. Even though the truck's cab was covered, the chilly mountain air still seeped through the cracks. Their grey woolen coats, some of them torn, didn't defend much against the cold.

After they were all piled in, Sgt. Rotz climbed onto the back of the truck and closed the hatch. Turning toward the cab of the truck, he hollered, "All set!" loudly enough for the driver to hear, and the truck began to rumble away from the camp.

The young prisoners sat quietly, wondering where they were being taken, when Max leaned over to Karl and half-whispered—something that was almost impossible given Max's deep voice—"The Americans liberated Mauthausen just a few days ago. It is a labor camp right outside Linz. They need a lot of help. Awful!"

Everyone could hear him, and they all listened intently, but nobody looked up or responded. The unspoken question lingered ominously in the air.

When was he there? Why had he not talked about this yesterday when he got back? Karl had noticed that he had been unusually quiet last evening; normally Max was the loudest, most obnoxious one in the room. But Karl had seen his silence at the time as a welcome break, and didn't want to question it.

As the truck continued to bump along, the boys repeatedly rubbed their hands over their crossed arms in hopes of generating some warmth. Karl was physically shivering, his teeth clattering from a combination of cold and worry. And the thought of innocent people being kept in these labor camps made the truck ride even colder. He would have to face these prisoners; but hopefully, his youth would protect him from their potential wrath. What had Hitler done to this country?

Max was still whispering. "Thousands and thousands were killed!" he was saying.

"Killed? They killed the prisoners? Only the worst offenders, right?"

"They killed thousands!" Max hissed. "Prepare yourselves. They took a few of us to Mauthausen yesterday morning. I saw piles and piles of skeletons, dead after dead. You will see a lot of sick, cripples, half-dead. Hitler did a horrible thing. Hitler cheated us, and he lied to us, all of us! And I am told there were many more camps. Apparently, Mauthausen was one of many camps to be liberated. The Russians have already liberated some others."

"Cripples?" Karl didn't want Hermann to be one of them there or in any camp.

"You there! Shut up! *Halt's maul*! They'll see it soon enough!" ordered Sgt. Rotz, waving his rifle at Max.

Max stopped talking, leaned back and took a deep breath. Sgt. Rotz's German was surprisingly better than everyone had expected. He seemed to understand more than he could speak.

The rest of the cold and bumpy twenty-minute ride was silent, until suddenly Max pointed through one of the cracks in the back of the truck, *"Look! Schau!"*

Karl turned around to peer through the wide crack behind him. The truck had arrived at the end of one side of a wall, stopping at a grey stone gate. Karl noticed the 'Nazi Eagle' sign carved out of rock on the ground—it no doubt had once hung above the entrance; but now it lay in pieces on the side of the gravel road.

"The eagle was pulled off by the camp prisoners," Max whispered, glancing sideways at Sgt. Rotz to see if he would shush him again.

They all continued to peer through the cracks in the cab as the truck rattled through the gate. There were a few people walking around inside the compound, and Karl held his breath. What was this? He had to look closely to make sure he knew what he was seeing.

These people were little more than walking skeletons, just skin and bones. Some limped around on crutches, with makeshift wooden sticks in place of feet that had at some point been amputated. Others just sat leaning against the building wall. All were wearing gray and blue-striped, pajama-like clothing.

The truck then passed a rock quarry, and Max whispered, "The guards made them break rocks." He pointed to the stairs that led up the quarry. "That was the *Todesstufe*, the Stairs to Death. They forced prisoners to repeatedly carry heavy granite blocks up those stairs until they died, or they were murdered if they failed."

"How do you know?" Frederick demanded.

"They told me this yesterday when I was here," Max countered defensively.

"*Who* told you?" Frederick pressed.

Sgt. Rotz leaned forward, close to Frederick's face. "He is right. That's what *your* Hitler did!" he hissed at Frederick in his broken German.

Frederick immediately looked down, feeling guilty that he was associated with Hitler at all just by being German.

Karl was aghast. *Nein, no that's not possible!* Despite seeing some of the atrocities with his own eyes, he still couldn't fully comprehend what he was witnessing.

But Max was right. The rock-quarry in Mauthausen was at the base of the infamous 'Stairs of Death'. Prisoners were forced to carry roughly-hewn blocks of stone, often weighing as much as fifty kilograms, up the one hundred and eighty-six stairs, one behind the other. Many exhausted prisoners collapsed in front of the other prisoners in the line, falling on top of the other prisoners and creating a horrific domino effect.

The Mauthausen concentration camp was the only one in Austrian territory. At the time of the largest expansion, at the end of March 1945, it consisted of five different camps, each with 8,000 to 10,000 prisoners. In the Mauthausen camp, between 95,000 and 100,000 people were murdered—they starved or froze to death, died of disease or exhaustion, were beaten to death, shot while trying to flee, suffocated in the gas chambers, or died via heart injections or were otherwise executed. [v]

Karl noticed the American flag blowing in the wind, where the Nazi flag undoubtedly hung just a few days ago. The Red Cross and medics had taken over managing the concentration camp. Together with the rest of the GIs and the help of young German prisoners of war, they had begun the arduous task of cleaning up the camp, burying the dead, and nursing the sick back to health before they could travel home. Where those homes were, however, was not immediately clear, since they had been corralled from all walks of life and from all corners of Europe.

The truck came to a rumbling halt. With the butt of his rifle, Sgt. Rotz nudged Max, who sat the closest to the exit. "Get down! *Runter!*" he ordered, and he gestured for all of them to get off the truck.

As soon as Karl jumped off, he was surrounded by a sweet odor in the air that burned his nose. He looked around. The eerie feeling that started in the truck was now overwhelming. Suddenly, he found it hard to breathe.

An older German civilian worker in worn-out blue overalls passed by them, his head hanging low and his face grim, leading a horse by its halter. The horse was pulling a buggy full of stacked corpses. Karl stared, holding his breath. He almost wanted to cover his eyes, but he forced himself to look on in disbelief and bewilderment.

At the other end of the building, two more civilian workers stood next to a stack of forty or so bodies. They were grabbing corpses on each end—one the arms, the other the legs—and swinging them one-by-one onto another buggy hooked up to a plow horse with its head down, waiting.

Further up the north end of the concentration camp, more civilian workers were digging graves for all these former prisoners who had died horrible deaths.

The stench was overpowering. It smelled like a burning smell mixed with the reek of dead flesh. Flies were buzzed everywhere. When

Karl looked closer, he could see rats feasting on some of the corpses. He had a hard time processing what he was seeing.

Karl pulled his dirty coat sleeve over his hand and covered his mouth and nose with it—not just to avoid the horrible smell. He wanted to wake up from this nightmare. His thoughts were racing. *What is this? What happened here?*

At first, he wanted to avoid it all and look away. It was all starting to sink in. He wanted it not to be true. He felt like he had entered a horror show, a nightmare so unimaginable, something he didn't want to be part of. Hitler and his followers had lied to an entire country. Only the few closest to Hitler could have known what was really going on.

"We need you to help dig the graves and help bury these bodies," Sgt. Rotz hissed harshly at them, as if they had any responsibility in what happened here. "Spades are over there."

The boys followed where his finger pointed, in the direction of where the graves were being dug.

Karl bit his lips and clenched his fists. Tears welled up in his eyes, but he forced them back. He tried to take a deep breath, but instead choked on the stench. Blocking out what he was seeing and ignoring any further thoughts of what had happened here, he grabbed a spade and mechanically started digging alongside others: German civilians, GIs, young POWs, and even former prisoners who were strong enough to help.

Germans from Linz and the surrounding villages were already walking the grounds; they had been ordered to come here to witness the atrocities and also to help clean up and dig the graves. Women with handkerchiefs in front of their faces walked by. Many were crying, all looked solemn. A few threw up.

Buggy after buggy delivered a new heap of bodies to the trenches, and the bodies were dropped into the open earth. A GI eventually used a mechanism Karl had never seen before, called a "crawler tractor", to help move the bodies into the grave and to help push the dirt over the bodies.

That evening, when Karl and the crew returned to their makeshift internment camp, nobody said a word. For the first time since the SS had come to get him to join the war, Karl cried himself to sleep.

The next morning Karl and the other boys were transported back to the camp, where they were tasked again with helping to bury the bodies north of the camp. Later in the morning, the boys again near exhaustion and completely starved, Sgt. Rotz tapped Karl, Max, Frederick, and Wilfried on their shoulders.

"You are coming with me."

Itching, dirty, fatigued and starting to feel his stomach turn again, Karl followed the group back to the front, to the first grey stone building in the concentration camp. They leaned their spades against the wall of the building they were about to enter, and then one-by-one stepped through the front door.

As Karl's eyes slowly adjusted to the dim light inside, he tried to comprehend what he was seeing. On wooden bunk beds along the wall, there were still hundreds of clothed skeletons. Except they weren't skeletons. They were moving—their heads were moving, staring directly at Karl through large, dark, hollowed eyes. Bunk after bunk was packed with the sick and the dying, with no room to spare.

"Here you do exactly what the Red Cross personnel tell you to do," Sgt. Rotz ordered Karl and the rest of the young prisoners of war in his broken German. Karl examined the group of young men wearing helmets marked with the Red Cross insignia. "They need your help. They will give you the orders, and you will follow them."

With his eyes fixed on the four young German prisoners, Sgt. Rotz continued pointing at the three Red Cross medics just a few feet away, who were patiently waiting for Rotz to finish. "They are in charge here. They are here to help the sick, to feed them, to clothe them, to heal them and to help them get better so they can go home. You are here to help the medics with anything they need. Understood?"

Two of the boys nodded. They still had not digested what they had witnessed over the last day, and were still too shocked to react quickly.

Sgt. Rotz was not happy with the slow, nonverbal response. He leaned in closer to them and screamed, specifically at Karl, "Do you understand!"

The young prisoners snapped out of their fog for a second, nodded and in almost unison answered, *"Jawohl,* Sergeant!"

One of the Red Cross guys stepped forward and introduced himself in a calm voice in fluent German. "My name is Marco Steiger. You can help fix the bunks and chairs; and you can help clean, cook, scrub. Some of the patients here have to be hand-fed; they are so weak they can't hold up their own bowls or spoons. They haven't had a full stomach in months or years. They need to be fed slowly and given tiny amounts of food and drink at a time. The human waste bowls have to be emptied; there is a liquid manure where it all can be dumped in the back. We will show you where.

"Many of the concentration camp victims here are near death. We need to nurture them back to health. The ones that don't make it, need a deserving burial. The last few days we have sent the acutely ill patients to the Linzer hospital for special and critical care, but it is over capacity now. We will need to transport the others to the Gusen hospital today. The Mauthausen hospital is disgusting and we can't take them there.

"Next door, we've also set up a makeshift hospital for the manageable and less urgent cases. Many are staying in their bunks until they get better; there is just not enough room for them all. The patients remaining here for treatment need to be made as comfortable as possible.

"Also, the bunks are stacked too closely in here. We need to take out the middle layer to give the sick more space to move around, and to give the medics better access. We can use the extra wood for heat and cooking. Some of the bunks are broken or chipped. All need to be fixed; we don't want the sick to get hurt further.

"Typhus is rampant. Rats and lice are everywhere. We need to scrub and scrub. When working here, wash your hands thoroughly and often. You do not want to catch typhus!"

This was the first time in as long as Karl could remember that an adult had talked to him in a civil, respectful manner, without giving orders, treating Karl as an equal.

Marco's eyes were bloodshot. It was clear he hadn't slept much since he had arrived here. He went on passionately about their plans to get everyone back to health and out of there as fast as possible. Karl was impressed by Marco's demeanor, and his determination was contagious. Karl was eager to help.

"I have carpentry skills," he volunteered. "I could help fix the bunks or chairs or anything you need fixed." Karl now knew specifically why he was here. His determination to help was masking the overpowering sickness he was feeling, and for a moment he forgot his nausea and his hunger pains. He could help make these sick people more comfortable. He was ready to roll up his sleeves and get to work. Whatever he could do to help them get better and get them back to their homes and families.

If they had any families left.

Sgt. Rotz angrily interrupted Karl's train of thought, and in his broken German he barked, "Listen, *Kraut*! You do exactly what they tell you to do, whether that's cleaning out the shit from these sick people or carrying out the trash. You do what you are told!"

Karl wished that the sergeant could see that he just wanted to help, though he could somewhat empathize with the sergeant's resentment toward them, considering what his country had done. Sgt. Rotz vehemently hated anything German, or "*Kraut*" as he called them, and Karl could only imagine the horrible experiences he'd had. He'd probably seen his comrades killed in combat and more.

I know I could help fix the bunks, I am good with wood, he defiantly thought, but he bit his tongue. Sgt. Rotz needed to calm down. None of the young POWs meant any harm—they were just young teenagers, hungry, tired, and really just wanted to be in a warm bed at home with their families.

Marco ignored Sgt. Rotz's outburst and responded directly to Karl. "Oh that's good. We need carpentry skills. What's your name?"

"Karl," was the reluctant response, as Karl carefully watched Sgt. Rotz's reaction out of the side of his eyes.

"Karl, why don't you go with Jim here," Marco pointed at one of the other Red Cross workers standing next to him who appeared to be in his early twenties. "He can explain all the carpentry help that's needed and where the hammers and nails and other tools he found are, right, Jim?"

Jim nodded as Marco turned to address the rest of the team, continuing in fluent German, "I am told all four of you have carpentry skills, right?"

Just then a large, fat rat scurried near Karl's feet. He reflexively jumped back a step to avoid it, while Jim ignored the critter as if it was part of the daily routine.

"You all could get started right away," he said. "There are many bunks to be fixed, and the middle bunks need taking down. We have more bunks than patients, removing some of the planks will give the sick more room. And some of the bunks are cracked—look at this one."

Jim grabbed a nearby board that had come loose and easily lifted it up. "This is way too dangerous for anyone to sleep on, especially for the fragile sick that are here. Some of the boards have nails sticking out and just need to be hammered in. Some of the chair legs are wobbly, and other repairs need to be made."

The men inspected the damaged furniture. After a short pause, Marco repeated, "The sick will be here for a while. At least until each is well enough to travel. We have to help them get better and make them comfortable in the meantime. And we could really use any extra wood for cooking and heating."

Jim tapped Max, Frederick and Wilfried on their shoulder. "You guys come with us. All of you can help with the woodwork with me and Karl." Jim said in his broken German, his brown eyes looking determined. "What are your names?"

They each responded in turn.

"Follow me. Let me show you the tool shed we've uncovered." With that, Jim marched ahead.

Sgt. Rotz started to tag along, stern and determined, but Marco stepped in between him and the assembled group and looked the sergeant firmly in the eyes.

"Jim's got this, he said calmly in English. "He can handle them. Robert here will take you to the kitchen. They need more help in there, with the food and cleanup. Can you get us some help there?"

Robert stepped forward—a tall, blonde worker in his early twenties, with friendly blue eyes.

Agitated, Sgt. Rotz hissed back at Marco, "Remember, they are all prisoners of war. They might try to run. You are now responsible for them!"

"Look at them; they are just kids, hungry and tired." Marco pointed at scrawny Frederick, who in his oversized, ripped coat looked more worried about his next meal than about escaping. "If it was up to me, they wouldn't even be here; I'd send them back home. I respect that you captured them as prisoners of war, but don't expect me to treat them poorly. I'll use their help, but that is it!"

Marco continued, just as agitated, "And where would they run to, anyhow? There is nothing for miles and miles, with the Russians on the other side."

Rotz just waved his rifle at the young captives, ignoring Marco's outburst. "Just go," he ordered them, irritation seeping from his voice. "Remember, all of you meet back at the truck exactly at 19:00."

"Yes, sir!" the prisoners responded.

With that, Jim slowly motioned to Karl and the rest of the group and said, "Let's go."

Meanwhile, Robert led Sgt. Rotz to the kitchen, and Marco went off to check on the other Red Cross workers. He had to welcome and coordinate other batches of helpers.

Jim and his newly-formed crew walked through the connected grey and dark buildings, only a few electric bulbs lighting up the hallways. Bunk after bunk covered the walls, with more skeletons on them—people just skin and bones, some laying down and resting, others sitting up with their heads in their hands watching the new arrivals.

"Water, please," a weak voice pleaded. It was one of the sick. "I am so thirsty."

It was an older patient, trying to sit up. His age was hard to judge as he was very malnourished. Karl guessed him to be around fifty. Jim walked over to tell him that the nurse would be back around soon with more water. The man laid back down and his head fell over, his eyes wide open; he didn't move again. Jim rushed over to take the man's pulse around the wrist for a minute. "Nothing! He is gone!" Defeated, Jim waved one of the medics over. "Take him out of here. He's done!"

Karl stared at the man in shock. Men were still dying in front of them by the hour. He felt helpless. He wanted to help so much more. Karl didn't dare to ask nor think about what that man had been through.

They kept walking past many more skeletal figures, most barely alive in a questionable state, until they heard another younger, whiny voice pleading, "Water, please. I really need water."

Jim slowly walked over to check on the desperate-sounding youngster and gently touched the malnourished kid's leg. "They will come around shortly and bring water and food for everyone. You had water less than an hour ago, right?"

The sick boy nodded slightly. He looked so malnourished that Karl wasn't sure why he hadn't been one of the sick who were transported to the hospital.

Karl looked closer; there was something about him that looked familiar. It couldn't be...

"Daniel?" The light was dim, and dark shadows fell over the wasted figure. His facial features were almost unrecognizable. The boy reacted slowly; his eyes, though open, seemed dead.

"You know him?" Jim looked at Karl inquisitively.

"I think so," Karl responded, continuing to stare at the sick boy, studying his face further.

Jim leaned in even closer to the boy and slowly picked up the bony hand to stroke it. Touching this boy or any of the sick was dangerous because any of them could have typhus, tuberculosis, and other such contagious disease. Many had lice.

Jim in his broken German continued to calm the boy: "You can't drink too much at once; your body has to get adjusted slowly. They will be back shortly with more water and food. You have to start eating and drinking slowly, otherwise you will get very sick, or you could even die."

Jim stroked the bony hand a moment longer, and then slowly put it back down on the wooden plank.

Jim moved back, and Karl took a step forward.

"Daniel?" he repeated, leaning down towards the figure. He was now almost certain it was Daniel. Their adventurous times together began flashing through Karl's mind. Soccer games behind their house, with makeshift goals, and many races run through forbidden wheat fields; Daniel helping out with all their chores, cutting trees and planting potatoes. Karl had been so busy with his own tumultuous life that he hadn't thought about Daniel lately, but now all his childhood memories with the boy were vivid. The Jewish friend who had asked Karl to help hide him! There it was again, the incredible feeling of guilt.

It's my fault.

Tears flooded into his eyes. He tightly squeezed the skin between his thumb and pointer finger. *No, do not cry.*

Daniel was barely recognizable: he was half his weight, with sunken, dead eyes, no hair. Was it completely shaven, or had his hair fallen out from malnutrition?

As Daniel looked back at Karl, his eyes attempted to smile weakly, as if finally recognizing him.

"Karl," he muttered barely. And then again, stronger, "Karl!" The surprise in his voice was clear.

Karl grabbed Daniel's hand and held it, tears again welled up in Karl's eyes. "Daniel, I am here! I am here to help you. I will help make you better. I am so sorry!" What horrors had Daniel had to endure here?

Karl never really knew what happened to them. Last he had heard, after Mr. Morgenthau was taken in for questioning and disappeared, Daniel and the rest of his family had gone to hide out at Mrs. Morgenthau's parent's house.

Karl had planned on visiting Daniel at his grandparents' house, but before he had gotten around to it, the SS had arrested the entire family at the grandparents' house and taken them away one Sunday evening. Albert's uncle had been leading the SS pack in the arrest, Karl learned later through Frau Müller and Mutter.

Guilt rushed over him. *What if I had not sent him away that night and instead just hid them all there and then?* But if the SS could track them down at the grandparents' house, surely the SS would have found them at Karl's also?

Mutter had mentioned rumors about labor camps, but nobody seemed to know more details. If they did, nobody talked about them. Mainly, even when he had heard the description of labor camps, Karl had imagined people being put to work, lots of work.

But never did he expect them to be death camps such as this.

"So this is where they brought you..." Karl whispered, now understanding why nobody could have known where the Nazis had taken them. Nobody in his village knew about Mauthausen. The grizzly puzzle was starting to fit together.

Jim stepped back in to try to help calm Daniel. "We have to fix some of the bunks," he said gently. "Karl has work to do, but my other colleagues will be around soon, I'll make sure of that. If I come back around and you still don't have water, I'll personally get you some, OK?"

The sick boy slowly laid his slightly lifted head back down.

"Karl," Daniel repeated one last time.

"What?" Karl responded holding his breath.

"Mom and Dad and my sister Anna are all dead. They were all murdered here." Daniel barely managed to say it. His cold eyes stared straight up at the ceiling.

Karl winced. The news felt like a punch to his stomach.

"*Mein Gott*, how horrible," he whispered, trying to lean back over Daniel. But that was all he said. He kept his real feelings inside. Karl really just wanted to scream. All the anger of the past months was culminating, mixed in with guilt and shame.

Controlling every nerve and emotion his body wanted to emit, Karl leaned forward again and promised, "Daniel, I won't ask any questions right now. Don't think about it now. Think about getting better—focus on yourself. You need to carry on the family legacy. I will make sure they take good care of you. You are now safe and in good hands. You are with the Americans; they will take care of you. Hitler killed himself. The war in Germany is over. They will get you better, and I'll make sure of that. Before you know it, you'll be back home. You will be out of here before me, so then please say 'hi' to Mutter for me." Karl's words were just pouring out of him, and he firmly believed that Daniel would be home before him. Who knew if Karl would ever see home again.

"We need to keep going," Jim gently cut in, breaking off the unlikely reunion. It was bittersweet, and Jim could hardly believe these two young men knew each other. But they all had a lot of work to do. Many more needed help here.

Karl gently touched Daniel's bony shoulder one final time and promised, "See you soon," leaning forward for a light hug, realizing Daniel was too weak to be grabbed.

"Don't!" Jim hissed. "Don't hug him! You don't want to get sick!" He gestured for Karl to follow him.

Karl followed Jim and the rest of the crew, who had been watching the interaction in silent amazement.

As Jim continued down the hall, Karl caught up and tapped his shoulder. "Could I get him and us some water?" he pleaded. "Could we also get him another blanket? He seems so cold!"

Jim turned around and studied Karl's face, recognizing the worried yet determined look. Then looking toward Daniel again behind them, Jim nodded his approval and pointed Karl in the direction of the former SS kitchen. Karl ran towards it.

In the kitchen he found armed guards huddling in the kitchen. Karl saw a water canister but didn't dare to take it.

"Who are you with? Where is your group?" one of the GIs in the kitchen immediately grabbed Karl's underarm.

"He is with me!"

Jim had known to follow Karl, because the young prisoner would not be allowed to roam alone without supervision. He was also worried about Sgt. Rotz's temper from the little interaction he had witnessed earlier.

The soldier looked at Jim, and before he loosed his grip, Karl angrily yanked himself loose. He was getting tired of being treated like a criminal; he just wanted to help. He didn't understand exactly what they were saying as they spoke intensely in English, but it clearly sounded angry. But Jim assured the soldier that all was fine.

The armed GI continued to explain himself to Jim, as if he felt bad that he was mean to Karl.

"We found a load of stored potatoes the SS had been hoarding. They let the prisoners starve but had several months' worth of potatoes here. We are guarding the supply because some of the former prisoners might come here and try to steal the potatoes, and eat themselves to death."

"Yes, they are eager to eat," Jim nodded. "We would be too! Some haven't had a full meal in years. Good to hear about this large potato supply. And we also have our military rations, so we are good. For now, though, this young man just needs some water."

The GI pointed to the faucet and water canisters and nodded his approval to Karl. Karl filled up a canister, and carried it back to Daniel. Without thinking, he started to hand the entire canister to his sick friend.

"No!"

Jim snatched the canister of water. Karl stared at him, bewildered. *What now?*

"He can only sip on this." Jim explained gently. "Remember, he will get really sick if he drinks too much or too fast. It could even kill him."

Karl turned back to Daniel. "Take it slow, only small sips. Your body is not used to this." Then he slowly lifted up Daniel's head and let him take a small, slow sip from the container. Some of the water spilled down Daniel's face and neck. Karl quickly wiped it off with his coat sleeve.

Daniel's deep-set eyes looked at Karl with so much warmth and appreciation that no words would have been able to express his thanks.

At that moment, Karl felt closer to Daniel than he ever had before, even while growing up and playing together in the same neighborhood. Back then they took each other for granted, and they were carefree, never questioning their freedom. Now they were reconnected, both having survived the war thus far in their own tragic ways.

Karl realized that, in comparison, the path his fate had taken him was tame compared to Daniel's, and who had been tortured here and had lost his family. He was only one year older than Karl, but he had aged many years physically through the horrendous treatment, and now his body was ravaged by starvation and disease. The emotional effect of all of that happened to him, Karl could not begin to comprehend.

Nobody's lives would ever be the same because of this war, but some lives were far more devastated than others.

"Don't you think a nurse should look at him?" Karl asked Jim, concerned. Now that he had found his friend, he didn't want to lose him again. "Could we find one of those Red Cross nurses I had seen walking around earlier? They need to diagnose him."

Karl felt responsible now for ensuring Daniel's recovery. *How could no one have found a way to hide his family in their village?* Karl asked himself for a moment but immediately knew the answer. It was nearly impossible to hide anyone in a small village. And nobody had really expected the Morgenthau family would be arrested and brought here. No one in his village even knew these camps existed.

"The critically ill have already been assessed and transported to the hospital. That means Daniel has already been examined. He will be fine. A few more weeks here and he will be good as new." Jim winked at Karl, trying to lighten the mood in one of the saddest situations Karl had ever found himself in.

Jim was eager to move on. He knew he couldn't get bogged down by one patient. There was too much to do; too many needed their help.

"Let's go now," he urged Karl after some time, "we have work to do." With that, the group of young POWs followed Jim again, leaving Daniel behind along with the many other patients, young and old, some in better health than others.

They walked in and out of buildings, passing a double crematory oven in the underground area between the hospital building and the bunker. They later found out that this oven had been installed just a few weeks before the concentration camp had been liberated.

The ovens were originally designed as baking ovens—Karl wondered if the makers of these ovens could have imagined what they would eventually be used for.

Other buildings were labeled "Shower Rooms." Jim stopped and pointed at them. In his broken German, he explained in a somber voice:

"Here was where the Nazis killed thousands. These 'shower rooms' were actually Zyklon-B gas chambers. Prisoners were lured into these rooms thinking they were just getting a shower. Instead they all were all brutally gassed."

Jim paused a moment before continuing. "After a while, people figured out that these weren't showers. But resistance was still futile. If you didn't go along, you would be tortured to death. Gassing was the quicker and less painful option."

Jim looked down and folded his hands in front of him as if to take a moment and pay respect in memory of the atrocities and all the innocent killed here. The young German prisoners also looked down. Karl felt that churning feeling return to his stomach—he felt like he was going to throw up. The fatigue, and trying to digest all he was seeing, was mentally and physically getting to be too much.

Jim reached for the door handle to one of the "shower" rooms, but then he noticed that Karl's face matched the color of the grey walls.

"Are you alright? You don't look too good."

Karl felt his knees collapse and held on to each to stabilize his body with both hands. His head nearly between his knees, he weakly tried to assure Jim that he was fine.

Jim put a comforting hand on Karl's shoulder.

"You will be fine," he assured the young soldier. "These were horrible atrocities Hitler and the Nazis have committed. You are too young; you could not have stopped anything. There was not much you four could have done, and if you would have tried you would have ended up in here or in one of the many other concentration camps throughout Europe I am hearing have been uncovered. Mauthausen is hopefully one of the last camps to be liberated!"

Jim was trying to console all of the teenagers. Frederick was leaning against the wall, silently crying, tears running down his face. He lowered himself, crumbling against the wall, and cried so hard his entire body shook. He wrapped his arms around his knees and buried his head in them. Max put his hand on Frederick's shoulder, while he also wiped tears from his own face with his sleeves. Out of the group of four, Max seemed to have himself most under control.

Jim still had his hand on Karl's shoulder, while Wilfried grabbed Karl's arm to try to help him stand up straight again. No one said a word.

"Follow me, let's just go outside for a minute and get some fresh air." Jim led them to the nearest door to take them outside.

The promised relief outside did not come for Karl. Instead, he felt he could smell the stench of burned and dead bodies in the air, just as when he first got here. The crematorium ovens had been out of service only a few days, and the creepy sweet stench was still lingering. The thin mountain air was trying to seep through and filter out what was left in the air of the horrible tragedy, but it would take months before the air was even somewhat fresh again.

Karl avoided taking deep breaths. The thought of particles of burned flesh still in the air revolted him. His body heaved, and he took a few steps forward into the middle of the gravel road and violently threw up. Because he had eaten so little for so long, he just kept gagging, throwing up green liquid bile. The raw nettles made their way back up.

When nothing was left to throw up, he dry-heaved and finally wiped his face with his sleeve. Then he just let himself fall down; he lay there in the collapsed fetal position. His entire experience, from the time they were taken in the middle of the night, to digging the trenches, to being commanded to the front, to now, and the unbelievable things he was witnessing, was more than the young man could handle. Karl sobbed uncontrollably.

Max tried to walk toward Karl, but Jim motioned him back, as if to say it might be best for Karl to be left alone and to just let it all out.

All the pain Karl had felt, all the fear and the emotions he had held in since the night the SS came to get them from Mutter's house was being released. Most of all, Karl couldn't believe how much he and his country had been deceived by the tyrant Hitler and his blind followers, the Nazis. How could he be from a country that was run by this tyrant and murderer?

Was a concentration camp where Hermann ended up? Where was Hans? Was he still alive? Was he in a Russian prison camp somewhere? Was he being tortured? How was Mutter doing? Opa? Did the Russians leave them be? Where was Uncle Joseph? He was overcome with shame. It was starting to sink in for the first time how the war had torn apart his family, his young life, his country. Germany was in ruins.

Max, Wilfried, and Frederick sat crisscrossed around Karl, all hanging their heads low and silently thinking their own worried thoughts, using their sleeves to wipe their tears here and there.

Karl eventually stopped crying, but remained on the ground, still overcome with anxiety and grief. He turned his head up and looked into the sky, his green eyes asking, *How could You let this happen?*

Even though Jim was part of the team of liberators, he empathized with the boys. He started to explain all that he knew about the background in his broken German. "The Nazis killed Jews and anyone trying to fight the regime. I've been told that they put them in camps like these all over Europe. Hitler wrote in his book *Mein Kampf* about his hatred for the Jews. He still blamed the Jews for signing the World War I treaty that heavily favored the enemies and ruined the German economy."

Karl looked up at Jim, shielding his eyes from the bright sun that was just above Jim's head. He appreciated the fact that this American knew what Hitler wrote in *Mein Kampf.*

Lifting his head, Karl responded slowly, in his best High German to make it easier for Jim to understand. Jim would have an impossible time comprehending Karl's Southern German Bavarian dialect.

"We were in the Hitler Youth. It was required of all teenagers to be part of it, and *Mein Kampf* was required reading. We discussed it at length at many of the meetings. Yet, we didn't know that Hitler was actually burning humans to death. That was never discussed. How sick, how mentally deranged!"

Karl slowly let his head fall back down, but at this point, he had no tears left to cry. The reality of all of it had sunk in, and he realized he needed to pick himself up now again and move on.

Jim was more understanding and patient than probably any other GI would have been. Here they were from two opposing countries, enemies in the war, talking and debating war crimes as if they were friends. Jim himself wasn't that much older than these teenagers, and luckily for the boys, he was very sympathetic to their plight.

But he also knew how much work there was to get done.

Karl sat up. He looked over and noticed a pile of paper sacks laying against the wall of one of the grey buildings. Jim followed his glance and pointed out that those paper bags had been used to dispose the dead bodies. Karl quickly looked away—he didn't want to get started again.

"We'd better go before Sgt. Rotz sees you sitting here. We are here to help the survivors. We need to nourish them and make them comfortable while they are healing. There are still dozens dying daily. The way you could make a difference now is to help the helpers, who are trying to help these people get them back on their feet! Let's fix the furniture, let's fix the bunks, and give the sick what they need, scrub everything. Let's make it as livable here as possible."

Karl slowly got himself up. Using his sleeve, he wiped away his last few tears and then straightened out his torn coat. Max, Frederick and Wilfried were already following Jim inside, and Karl slowly joined them. On the way in, Karl noticed the large blackened chimney of the crematorium. He stared at it for a second—he couldn't even fathom the type of people who blindly followed these orders to kill hundreds and thousands this way. How mentally sick and brainwashed, and possibly even scared, they themselves must had been. How did they justify this to themselves? How could they go home to their families? What would they tell them at the end of a work day, if anything?

Karl shook his head and walked on. He didn't want to think about it all for another minute; he knew he would get sick again. He needed to stay healthy to be able to help. And he didn't want to become a burden.

The group followed Jim to the front of a large majestic oak closet; Karl fleetingly admired the excellent carpentry work of the chiseled floral design on its face. The boys watched as Jim reached for the keys already in its doors, unlocking the doors and pulling them open. Neatly lined up in it were saws, hammers, screwdrivers, hundreds of different sized nails and screws, and anything one would need for fixing the bunks, chairs and other furniture.

Having regained control over his feelings, Karl's focus had shifted to helping the Red Cross workers heal the sick. His determination was renewed. He felt as if he had a purpose again.

Jim led the boys back through the barracks and pointed at several bunks that needed to have boards removed. They marveled again at the absurdly cramped quarters. Nurses would have to crouch down and virtually crawl under, or climb on top of, the bunks to get to some of the patients.

The boys quickly got to work. They began to hammer and saw away at the bunks. They completed one bunk after another and then moved on to the next. There was enough work to keep all four busy for weeks.

I wonder how long it will take to get everyone healthy here; how long will it take to clean up? Karl wondered whether he would ever be allowed to return home.

"Karl?"

Karl stopped sawing to look up to see Daniel right there. Karl hadn't realized they had come back to the same area they had left him before; they had come in through a different door, and all of the bunks looked the same in the dim lighting.

"*Ja*, Daniel?"

Karl knew he was supposed to work, but didn't see any harm in responding to Daniel.

"Where is Hans?"

Karl stopped for a second before he responded, "I don't know, Daniel."

"What about Hermann?"

"I am not sure."

"Did you ever hear from your Uncle Joseph again?"

"No, nothing."

"How are your Mutter and Opa?"

"I think they are at home, but I am not sure. I haven't seen them since October last year."

"What month is it now?"

"It's May 1945, Daniel."

Daniel just stared, his face empty of emotions.

"Daniel, it's probably best if you rest now and don't talk that much. I also have to work. I am an American prisoner of war. I surrendered to the GIs because I didn't want to be captured by the Russians. There is so much more I want to tell you, but it will have to be later. I have to work, or I will get in trouble. And I won't be able to hear you when I start sawing again, OK?"

With that, Karl continued his work. It was his way of blocking out the pain he felt now for Daniel and his family, and for himself, not knowing about his brothers, Mutter, Opa, Uncle Joseph, and all the others who suffered or died here.

Using his arms behind his head to prop it up, Daniel watched Karl saw away, too weak to sit up.

"How are you a POW? You are too young to be a soldier. Did you fight for the Nazis?" he asked when Karl's sawing paused for a moment.

Karl avoided eye contact with Daniel. He didn't want to explain too much at that point, so as to not upset Daniel.

"I had no choice. Hitler pulled in young and old in those last months. But you need to rest, Daniel! We'll talk later when you feel better and are stronger. I'll be back here tomorrow. Every day here you will get stronger."

Karl busied himself with sawing the board on the middle bunk right next to Daniel's bunk. Max soon joined Karl, pulling in tandem on the other end of the saw. Once they finished sawing, together they carried the boards out. They made a woodpile outside for the pieces to be used as firewood. They sawed and evened out some of the uneven posts, and sanded down others.

"Now, take these buckets and fill them with water and soap. Each one of the bunks in here needs to be scrubbed down. Here, take these rags," Jim directed Wilfried, handing him a metal bucket and a rag. "Once you are done scrubbing bunks, the nurses need help washing the patients!"

Karl and Max spent the rest of the day hammering, sawing, moving wooden boards, and repeating, bunk after bunk.

How much pain these bunks have seen, how much suffering and death. How many have died in these bunks? Karl didn't want to think about it anymore. Ignoring the blood splattered on some of the boards, he kept hammering and sawing, sweat pouring down his face and body. Then, when the sun started to set, they were told it was time to go back.

At exactly 19:00, Jim led them to the idling truck by the gate. Sgt. Rotz already stood impatiently outside, waiting to take his POWs back to their internment camp for the night.

Exhausted and back in their barracks, the boys were fed watery soup and dried bread, and shortly afterwards they retired to their rooms to sleep. Nobody spoke. They were all lost deep in their own thoughts.

The next day they were once again shuttled back to the concentration camp. Jim handed them buckets and directed them towards the water and soap in the former prisoner kitchen. That day, more help was needed to scrub the quarters and further disinfect everything. Dirt, bugs, sometimes even blood and other bodily fluids seemed to be everywhere. Here and there, Karl saw more rats darting about.

Karl took a rag and dipped it into the scalding hot water—his hands almost burned. They had been instructed to use the hottest water available. He wrung out the suds of the rag and started to wipe down bunk after bunk. He wondered if the prisoners had ever at one point cleaned the bunks themselves.

But after a while, they all were too weak to clean, and the captives must not have cared. That's probably how the diseases started.

Karl couldn't even imagine the day-to-day activities of a prisoner here before they were liberated. His thoughts raced through his mind as he scrubbed.

How could they even sleep after a hard day's work in the rock quarry, with hardly any food in their stomach, and all that worry about dying any day? The worry alone must have been torture! Did they become too weak to care after a while?

Some of the sick gave Karl a smile of thanks; others who felt stronger patted him on the back. Karl found that he really enjoyed doing this work, and he felt he was finally somewhat useful.

After they were done scrubbing down the bunks, Jim told Karl and Max he needed help again to continue fixing the bunks. The list of tasks to be completed truly was endless.

At one point, after a few weeks, the GIs realized that they were losing the fight against the various diseases. All the cleaning hadn't helped—typhus and tuberculosis still raged, and the bugs and rats just couldn't be eradicated fast enough. The sick were still dying daily. They decided the only way to contain them further was to burn down some of the infected smaller buildings.

So a few camp buildings were burned down using a controlled fire, and Karl was a bit discouraged that all their scrubbing, fixing and working on the bunks in those buildings had been in vain.

The remaining buildings had to then be sterilized more thoroughly than before.   Together with other German civilians who were ordered to the camp daily to help, the four young POWs cleaned and scrubbed with new fervor. When the nurses needed more help with the sick, they cleaned out bedpans and helped wash, clean, and feed the patients. Often when cleaning them, Karl had to dab around their scabs and wounds carefully.

I don't even want to know how they got these, he often thought. He avoided the questions and remained cheerful with each of them—he knew he couldn't handle the explanations of how they each got their scars and often still-open wounds.

Their daily tasks started to become routine. Karl made it a point each day to stop by and visit Daniel just for a few minutes—more wasn't allowed. They were ordered here to work and not to socialize. Sgt. Rotz had made that clear.

But Karl always made sure Daniel had enough water, enough food, and made sure to give him anything he needed. If Daniel felt cold, Karl would find him more blankets and made sure the doors were closed to keep the cool air out. If he was hot, Karl ran to open the door to let fresh air in. A few times, the two boys reminisced briefly about the good times growing up together in their neighborhood.

Of course, Karl couldn't give Daniel back his family, which was what he would have needed most to heal faster. Karl completely avoided that topic, and didn't bring up what happened to Albert. Karl also didn't talk of his worries about his own family. He wanted Daniel to focus on the positives to help him heal. Later, once Daniel was stronger again, there would be plenty of time to go into those traumatic details if needed. The immediate goal was just to get Daniel healthy.

In reality, Karl would not talk about his experience in Mauthausen for another next twenty years.

At the end of the first week, Daniel was able to sit up on his own. With the help of a Red Cross nurse, he even took a couple of steps. Daniel seemed to be well on his way to recovery. On the following Wednesday, to Karl's surprise, Daniel smiled bigger than usual at him.

"Come closer," he whispered. And when Karl curiously leaned in, Daniel slowly pulled out a chocolate bar from behind his back. Karl laughed, hard; he thought Daniel was like a magician pulling a rabbit out of his hat. And in that moment, Karl realized that it was great to be able to laugh again.

"Here, I've saved this for you." Daniel proudly handed the chocolate to Karl, with the biggest grin Karl had seen on Daniel since they were reunited.

"*Schokolade!*" Karl read the label. "Hershey's Chocolate!" and he grabbed the desired sweets. "Oh *danke*, Daniel, *danke*! I haven't eaten chocolate in years."

"Hide it!"

"I will," Karl promised, shoving the bar into his coat pocket, looking around to make sure that nobody had seen this interaction. A few of the sick might have seen it, but if they did, they had looked away and didn't say anything. Shortly after, barely able to contain his excitement, Karl snuck into the camp bathroom and savored the treat inside the stall. He let the chocolate melt in his mouth. He didn't want anyone else to see or possibly envy his bounty. He certainly didn't want to share this first chocolate bar he had eaten in years. He decided then and there that Hershey's chocolate would be his favorite forever.

Though Karl had to overcome his disgust for working in the concentration camp environment, and all it stood for—as well as cleaning out the messy bedpans and vomit that often made his stomach turn—he started to look forward to his daily visit with Daniel, his only connection to home. Daniel now always saved chocolate bars and other treats for Karl.

The news of the liberation of yet another horrid camp had spread, and the food trucks were supplying the camp with much-needed nourishment for the sick on a regular basis. They also had to know that chocolate made anyone happier, and a happy person heals faster. Karl was certain.

Hunger was no longer an issue for the boys. Sgt. Fritz had been right when he first told Karl about the assignment. The sick were being fed well by the Red Cross with the potato stash that had been uncovered, and the various food supplies that were pouring in. The sick also sneaked chocolate and crackers and other food to the boys as gratitude to the boys for helping them get better. Whether it was cleaning out their bedpans, helping them to the bathroom, shower, or bringing them cooked meals, they were thankful for everything these young soldiers did for them.

But while Karl and his team ate well, hunger remained a huge problem for his German POW mates back at the internment camp. Karl wished he could take back some of the extra food to the campmates who had been left behind, but he was not allowed to take any food supplies back with them. At the end of each workday at the concentration camp, Karl and his comrades were searched before being taken back, to make sure they were not bringing with them any food. The concern was that food from the camp could be contaminated, and might spread the diseases rampant in the concentration camp to the barracks where the rest of the German POWs were being held.

Karl was immensely thankful for his job. Using his carpentry skills, he could make the sick feel more comfortable and aid in their healing. And he could personally tend to his childhood friend. He still marveled at the chances of him finding Daniel here. Surely it was a sign of good things to come.

One day, Daniel told him about how he witnessed a few cripples being euthanized here. Their only "crime", he said, had been that they were handicapped. He began to sob as he relived how horrible it was to watch those helpless being killed.

"Sssshhhhhh!" Karl put his finger to his lips, trying to comfort the distraught boy. "Please, for now, let's not talk about it anymore!"

Karl had heard and seen enough of the unspeakable gruesomeness. In hearing about the cripples, he couldn't help but worry even more about the whereabouts of Hermann, and, of course, Hans, Mutter, Opa and his uncle. Would he ever see them again?

With the constant worry at the back of his mind, he continued his daily labor. But on this day, an unusual itch slowed him down. It was an itch that just didn't want to stop, starting first on his scalp, and then his arms. Then he itched all over, scratching himself non-stop until Jim told him to stop.

"You've got lice," Jim told him. ""Don't scratch; it won't help."

Neither Jim nor any of the other workers were really surprised when Karl got lice, because most everyone already had them.

It was difficult not to scratch, and back at the internment camp that night Karl could not sleep at all—the pain kept him awake. The next day, back at the concentration camp, he asked a Red Cross nurse for advice on what to do about the lice, but he didn't get a good answer. Then, Karl got an idea.

He recalled all the large paper sacks that were lying around against the camp's walls that had originally been used for disposing of the dead bodies. That day, he tracked them down and decided to sleep in nothing but one of these 'body sacks' each night. While it didn't contribute any warmth, it helped keep the lice that were nesting in his clothes away. Despite hand-washing all the clothes, it had been impossible to get rid of them quickly.

Getting rid of the ones nesting in his hair was another ordeal. Karl showered and scrubbed himself more than ever; he requested a razor from Jim to shave his head completely bald. Watching his red curly hair drop on the floor, he hoped to get rid of the pest.

But like wildfire, the lice spread, and before too long all his roommates at the internment also had them. How fast they spread! The roommates requested he bring them back some of these paper bags and Karl got approval from Jim to take more back to the POW camp for the rest of his roommates to sleep in them. The thought that these paper bags were reserved for corpses was quickly pushed aside in favor of ridding themselves of the itchy pests.

The lice kept Karl scratching every inch of his body into his thirtieth night in American captivity. He once again got barely any sleep with the tiny bugs crawling all over him. And in the early daylight the next morning, before getting ready for yet another truck ride to the concentration camp, he could see he had red blotches all over his arms and legs. He was tired and cold, his bald head was itching, and his skin was burning. He rushed over to grab his clothes and got dressed as fast as he could, testing his self-control by not scratching, knowing it would make the itching only worse. He was the last one to get to the truck.

When he arrived at the concentration camp, he headed straight for Daniel's bunk, as was the daily routine. When he got there, however, Daniel's bunk was completely cleaned out with not even a blanket on it. Karl stared, baffled.

Where could Daniel be? Were his blankets and pillow being washed? Was Daniel at the latrine, or showering?

He decided to check back in a few minutes. By now, Daniel had regained much of his strength, and could move around on his own, though he still needed a cane. Perhaps he really was just at the latrine.

But when Karl checked back on him a few minutes later, Daniel's bed was still empty.

A worried feeling overcame Karl.

What happened to Daniel? He seemed healthy yesterday morning!

Karl sought out Jim. "Could you find out where Daniel is?"

"Sure," Jim agreed, and he and Karl walked back to near Daniel's bunk. Jim called over one of the young blonde Red Cross nurses who happened to walk by.

"The guy that was in that bunk bed over there, the young kid named Daniel, do you know where he is?"

The exhausted-looking nurse thought for a minute, then blew her blonde bangs out of her face "Yes, Daniel. Late last night he came down with a really bad fever. They suspected typhus, and they immediately transported him to the hospital in Linz."

"Typhus?" Karl cried. "But he was feeling better!"

Chapter 9

Ruins

Day after day, Karl pleaded with Jim to drive him or even let him walk the five kilometers to the nearby Linz hospital to see Daniel. Karl promised he would be back within two hours, at most; he just wanted to confirm Daniel was alright. He had lost his friend once already, and he didn't want to lose him again.

But Jim and the American GIs disapproved. Karl shouldn't be on his own that long—he was, after all, still a POW. And they had more important things to take care of than wasting time at the nearby hospital looking for a patient whom they were not even sure was there. Daniel could have easily been taken to any other hospital in the adjacent towns because the Linz hospital had already been filled to capacity months ago.

Irritated, Karl had gone to Marco to complain. "Don't you keep any types of records of the whereabouts of the sick?"

"Who has time to take detailed records of everyone? Our goal is to get the people here better," Marco snapped. He was also getting crankier as his time here went on. Seeing all the death and sickness, taking care of all the deathly ill while they were still dying daily, was taking its toll. "Let the historians sort out all the names and record keeping of what happened here."

Karl was getting desperate. He asked if anyone who had to go to the hospital, maybe even one of the nurses, could find out for him whether Daniel Morgenthau was there. Marco vaguely assured Karl that he would see what he could do. It did not sound promising. Daniel was Karl's last connection to his home. Lately, Karl had dreamed of them possibly even leaving the camp together. He had imagined how happy people on their suburban streets would be to see them both walk back home down their *Reichsstrasse.*

But now Karl wondered when or if he would ever see home again. What would home look like? Would there be a home? Had it been bombed like many of the neighborhoods in Linz? He had witnessed first-hand the destruction in Linz, and he had heard about all the bombings of other German cities—the dead, the fires, the ruins and the homeless. Now that the war was over, citizens were allowed to listen to the Allied radio stations again, and news of the bombings and devastation had traveled fast.

Daily, Karl and the young POWs continued to be shuttled to the concentration camp to do various chores. Continued hammering, fixing, cleaning, and tending to the sick. Yet after months of hard work, the number of patients remaining in the camp was still steadily shrinking.

The bodies had been buried, and the sick that couldn't walk on their own or were in bad shape had been shuttled to hospitals, or sent to temporary lazarets the GIs had set up. But even these lazarets and the hospitals started to clear out. Many prisoners had been cured, but many more had died, even after the liberation. They had been too sick or too weak to recover from diseases like typhus or tuberculosis. The 90,000 to 100,000 people recorded as murdered in Mauthausen did not account for the thousands who died after the concentration camp liberation.

But a good number did recuperate, and some even walked out on their own. Even if not completely healed, they were eager to go home, often with nothing but the striped clothes on their bodies. [1]

Karl continued to puzzle over how many people had stayed quiet about the existence of this camp. The Germans living in distant villages or cities, like his own family, could not have known; or they would not have believed it even if they were told. But those in the surrounding areas—they must have known something. They had to see and or smell the smoke. And yet they stood by and just looked away? It was all unfathomable to Karl.

General Eisenhower during his visit to Mauthausen right after the liberations had ordered soldiers to film the atrocities, and Marco, Jim, Sgt. Rotz and other GIs agreed that they wanted the remaining buildings to be maintained for historical reasons, as a reminder of all that had happened here for generations to come.

The group of teenage German POWs at the internment camp was getting smaller, too, Karl realized. He had been told that one group of the German POWs had been handed over to the Russians, and another group was handed over to the French. He was hearing that the Allied soldiers—the Americans, the Russians, and the French—

[1] Karl later learned that the German population didn't really want to deal with or hear about the concentration camp prisoners. To empathize with them would have been an admission of guilt—of knowing and not doing anything about it, or worse, guilty of contributing to the atrocities. Sympathy was not developed until decades later, when the new generations of Germans learned about the details of the atrocities.

were going to split up Germany. And Linz was on the eastern side, which meant that Russia would possibly take over this area.

Karl shuddered at the thought of being handed back over to the Russians. He wondered if the Red Cross could arrange it so that he and his *Kameraden* could be allowed to go home instead. He would even volunteer to stay and work for the GIs if that meant he wouldn't be handed over. He had been through enough; he couldn't imagine surviving the terror at a Russian POW camp.

****

One October morning, while Karl was getting ready for his daily shuttle to the concentration camp, before he could head out the door, Sgt. Rotz marched into their room and stood in the center of it, hollering, "You are leaving today. A train is taking you on your next journey!"

In the same commanding tone he would use for any other order on any other day, Sgt. Rotz continued, "The truck waiting outside will take you to the train station!"

Karl and his bunkmates could not believe what they were hearing. *What did this mean? Take a train to where? Home? Russia?*

It was easy for them to get ready and pack. They had nothing but the clothes on their backs.

The date was October 11, 1945—a year after the SS had taken Karl from his home, and over five months after he and Alois had surrendered to the Americans on that dirt road near the railroad crossing.

"Where will the train take us?" he dared to ask, still worried that they would be handed over to the Russians, as other captured teenage SS had been.

Sgt. Rotz did not answer.

"Move! *Schnell, schnell*, get out of here!" he ordered.

The fact that he didn't respond worried Karl even more. Without a word about their quandary, they were all ordered to get on the same truck that had been taking them to their daily cleanup and carpentry tasks at the concentration camp.

Today, however, it took them straight to the train station in Linz. As always, Sgt. Rotz was on the truck; but today he was there to ensure they got on the train.

"That train on track one is the one you all get on," he directed, pointing at the waiting train. Karl studied the train. It was facing east, and Karl prayed it did not take them to Russian territory. The words written on the side of it read "German State Railway". The only cars it pulled were those for transporting animals—cattle cars. Karl was sure that this was one of the many trains that had brought prisoners to Mauthausen. For a minute, he wondered about the kind of men and women who were responsible for the transports of all those innocent lives, and the kind of men who actually drove the locomotive. They had all contributed to the atrocities committed in Mauthausen. How did they justify transporting these prisoners? What about the men who shoveled the coal into the train's ovens to keep it moving? What about the many other railroad workers who maintained the tracks or took part in the prisoner transports? There were so many contributors, so many small cogs in the wheel that had all contributed directly and indirectly.

But everyone needed a job to support their families, and if one refused to do the work they were trained to do, no matter the consequences to other lives, they would have ended up unemployed with no other major skills, unable to feed their family. Worse, refusing an order could have landed them in the concentration camps with the rest of the prisoners.

The options had been dismal: to sacrifice oneself to save lives or to stay quiet and live.

Karl again wondered what his dad would have done if he had been alive during this time. Would his name be added to the list of those who vehemently tried to fight the regime and ended up being killed? Or would he have faithfully done his job, regardless of the effect on thousands of other lives?

The whistle of a train broke Karl out of his thoughts. They were filing onto the train, now. With an armed Sgt. Rotz hovering over them, the young POWs didn't have much choice but to hop on. The train had no convenient steps to climb—without them, how did the kids and elderly people get on and off this train? How many more fell and were injured?

Once they had all finally filed into one of the cattle cars, Sgt. Rotz slammed the big metal doors shut with a thunderous bang. Karl was sure this was the last he would ever see Sgt. Rotz, and he would not miss him one bit.

Another loud thud, and they could hear the lock fall into place, signifying the end of Karl's chapter in American POW captivity, and the beginning of the unknown future that awaited him.

With a rumble, the train pulled forward. Karl and the other POWs all fell silent. If it wasn't for a few little rectangular windows lining the top of the wagon, it would have been completely dark inside.

Overall, the GIs had been good to Karl, he reflected. They had saved him from the Russians, and a much worse fate that would have awaited him with them—he would never forget the Russians killing his comrades in that wide open field.

But in American captivity he had been fed, clothed, and he had been able to contribute and help clean up the aftermath of Mauthausen. Karl considered it a privilege that he had been allowed to help nurse the sick back to health and make them feel more comfortable. And he had been able to witness the outcome of the Nazi atrocities that, had he not seen it for himself, he was not sure he would have believed if anyone had just told him about it.

Karl glanced at the other boys. He had become close friends with Frederick, Max, and Wilfried, and he knew they would meet again someday. He had found Daniel, too, and then lost him again. Fate had crossed their paths in Mauthausen under the worst of circumstances. He continued to wonder about Daniel's disappearance from the camp, and was still determined to find out what had happened to him.

Karl and the other former POWs took turns standing on the tip of their toes, pushing and shoving each other trying to get a better look out the tiny train windows.

The railroad workers couldn't have known what was happening to the prisoners at the camp, could they? They must have suspected something. Or maybe the coal workers loading coal onto the train were prisoners themselves, forced to do the work. Karl had a hard time comprehending how so many could not have known about what was happening to the prisoners.

Could the locomotive driver have somehow saved them and taken the prisoners somewhere else to freedom? But to where? There had been plenty of spies everywhere during that time, who would have reported any missing train immediately. It would not have ended well for anyone involved.

Karl sat back down on the hard, straw-covered floor of the cattle car, crammed in with his comrades. So many questions ran through his mind. *I wonder if our locomotive driver is the same who drove the prisoners. Or did the Americans arrest them and this driver is new? What are the perpetrators doing now? Where are they?*

Even with the dim light, Karl noticed dark stains splattered on the wall of the train cab, and he knew it had to be the dried blood of the concentration camp prisoners. He wondered how many prisoners had died during the transport alone.

Karl shook the thought away. He needed to get his mind off all of this. Jumping up to join some of the others staring out the window, he imagined breathing in fresh air, and what he would give to smell the resin-filled air in his Opa's carpentry. He so badly wanted to be home.

The boys continued to take turns gawking at what passed by outside. The train continued to pass through numerous small train stations and small towns whose names they didn't recognize. Whenever they could see a train station's name, they hollered it out. But while the train slowed down when it got close to some of the larger train stations, and they got excited over and over again, the train never completely stopped. If they could only pry open the doors, they could jump out.

Sitting in their tiny cramped space, they went around the cabin, and each started talking about home. They were surprised to learn that they were all from the same areas surrounding Nürnberg. But since none of them had ever been to Linz in Austria before captivity, they weren't familiar with this part of the country, and they still could not determine with certainty where exactly they were heading. They were starting to become more hopeful that they were going home, though—the GIs must have put them all on the same train because they were from regions near each other.

Or was that just a coincidence?

As the train continued to rattle across the German countryside, the boys could see grassland, fields, hills, valleys, forests, cattle, and some horses. But most unnerving to see were the buildings on fire, and smoke rising high into the skies. The devastation was vast. Germany lay defeated. Everyone looked on in shocked awe as the scenes slowly passed by. Nobody said a word, each thinking their own thoughts of how Germany could have ended up like this, in rubble. The lives they had known before the war would forever be gone. The Germany that used to be known for its poets, engineers, musicians, and other great accomplishments, was now known for starting two world wars.

It must be the most hated nation in the world now, Karl thought grimly.

"We are going further east," one of the younger boys suddenly cried out in fear and confusion, breaking the silence. He didn't look much older than fourteen. Was he right? Were they heading for Russia? It would take days to get there, though. And they had no food, no water. If they made it there alive, they would never see home again. Of that, they were convinced.

A few of them got together to try to pry open the doors again, squeezing their fingertips into the tiny metal space until they swelled and turned red, but the exit was securely locked from the outside. The camp prisoners transported in here surely would have tried the same, and none had succeeded. The door and locks were unbreakable.

They sat back down again, feeling defeated.

And then.

"Passau!" one of the boys peering out the window screamed. It was finally a station they recognized. They all jumped up to stare outside in excitement—but the excitement quickly turned into astonishment.

"Look there! And look here!" It was all Karl heard. He squeezed next to the boys and pressed his face against the corner of one of the windows to see what their bewilderment was about.

He clearly saw even more of the shocking destruction: train tracks bombed, parts of the train station building crumbled. The area was devastated.

How long will it take to rebuild all of this?

Karl stared, aghast, as he watched people—mostly women and old men—laboring away at removing the debris. It could be assumed that most of the younger men had died in the war, or were injured or captured and couldn't help. The rebuilding of Germany by the battle-worn and remaining Germans had begun; digging it out from under the rubble would take years.

The train slowed down to a crawl as it approached the station. Karl wondered if it would have to come to a complete stop—the train tracks were impassable.

But the train eventually moved past Passau without coming to a complete stop, and slowly sped up again, roaring on. Soon it would have to pass through Nürnberg. And Karl dared to hope again.

"Hopefully," he thought aloud, "the train stops in Nürnberg so we all can get off and finally go home. I can walk to my house from there."

"I'll get off anywhere it stops now. We can hitchhike or walk home from anywhere near Passau," one of the boys replied.

They all agreed. They were in familiar territory now. And they had been on this train for over three hours now, without any food or water all day. They were ready just to jump off, if only those doors would open.

"I can't take this much longer!"

"Me either!"

"The war is over. They should let us out!" Karl chimed in.

Some of them began banging their fists and kicking their feet hard against the door. As Karl watched them, he suspected many of the concentration camp prisoners transported in this same train car had tried the same. But, just as it had been for those prisoners, it was useless now. Nobody could hear them. The train was much too loud. And the driver had his orders, and would follow them no matter what these boys were demanding.

They were anxious for the train to reach Nürnberg, which they knew had to be the next big city. They would have to be let out then. After that, the train tracks could only lead further toward the Russian demilitarized zone, and then they would for sure end up in Russian captivity.

After what seemed an eternity of sitting helplessly, mixed with standing to eagerly look out the window, one of the boys screamed: "Nürnberg! Nürnberg! Nürnberg!"

All of them jumped up again to squeeze around the holes to the outside, desperate to catch a glimpse. It had been almost a year since Karl had last seen home. So much had changed for him. He had witnessed things in his young life that nobody in any lifetime should have to see.

But would the train stop?

The brakes were squealing. The train was now slowing down.

Through the narrow windows they could see a Nürnberg that lay in ruins. Destroyed railroad tracks, crumbled homes. In the far distance, the Nürnberg Cathedral's St. Lorenz church's tower stood half-demolished. The Nürnberg old town was decimated.

Here, women and children were laboring away in the ruins, removing the rubble from the tracks. Broken cinder blocks were passed down a chain of women standing lined up on a pile of rubble; piece-by-piece, the blocks were placed in a wheelbarrow and wheeled off to be dumped further down the road onto a growing pile of rubble.

Karl had seen enough. He started banging so hard on the metal door, the skin on his knuckles cracked and began to bleed. "They need to let us out!" he cried, feeling panicked and helpless. He needed to get out of here—now. This was his only chance to finally be free.

He needed to find out whether his family had survived the bombings. Was Hans home? Did he make it back? What about Hermann? Uncle Joseph? Daniel? He missed them all so very much.

One of the other boys started to scream, "Let us out!"

And one after the other, they all joined in shouting, "Let us out! Let us out!"

With a long, loud screech, the train came to a halt. The boys looked around in disbelief, and then started cheering. They stared in anticipation at the locked door.

Were they going to open the door? Would they let them go?

They began hollering in unison. "Open the door! Open the door!"

"Shhhh!" one said suddenly, putting his fingers in front of his lips. Everyone quieted down.

Something was rattling outside their cattle car doors. Someone on the outside seemed to be working the lock.

With one loud pull, the doors snapped open, and daylight poured in. Their eyes adjusted to seeing the locomotive driver standing in the doorway.

"Welcome home!"

He stood there in his coal-blackened uniform with his arms wide open, flashing a wide yellow-toothed smile. He knew this finally meant freedom for the boys.

It was the end of the line for this train—the tracks were so severely damaged, it couldn't have gone any further—and it was also the end of the line for these boys. Their time of witnessing one of the most gruesome chapters of history had come to an end.

As fast as they could, one after the other, they jumped off the train. They were finally free.

Chapter 10

Flight back

Karl opens his eyes.

Slowly he looks around and sees an IV stuck in his arm, a thin hose leading to a drip. His chest is covered in probes that are connected to a heart monitor, and he registers its rhythmic beeping.

He lifts his head off the white hospital pillow and sees Ellie lying in a cot next to him, still asleep. She had insisted on spending the night with him here.

He is in the American hospital in Virginia. They brought him here last night because of his heart issues, he recalls now, wide awake. *Boy, what a good night's sleep*, he muses. The jet lag really did him in. Or was it the new medication? Probably both.

Dr. Schlesinger had insisted he spend the night here. And with the help of one of his health insurance representatives, Ellie has Karl on a *Lufthansa* flight back to Frankfurt later today, leaving Dulles at 17:00. He will be flying first class, and an ambulance will be waiting for him at Frankfurt airport. Dr. Schlesinger has given clear written instructions for Karl's health insurance, and his German doctors can't ignore Karl's health needs any longer, even though he is seventy-five. His heart medication needs to be adjusted, and a stent needs to be placed as soon as possible.

Karl exhales deeply as he senses he is in good hands.

Dr. Schlesinger had told Ellie last night that she is a bit concerned about Karl's long overseas flight, but Karl insists he does not want to have surgery in a U.S. hospital—he wants to be at home if there is any chance of dying. Dr. Schlesinger warned that he needed the surgery as soon as possible, and that he is definitely traveling at his own risk. But since he insists on going, Karl will need to continue taking the new set of blood thinner medication she has prescribed. Karl is somewhat concerned about his diagnosis, but at the same time, he is grateful that a cardiologist with her impressive credentials has taken the time to give him a more detailed check-up for once. *Socialized medicine*, he thinks and shakes his head. Ellie is right: in the U.S., as long as you can pay for it, the doctors will take care of you. Though in the case of Dr. Schlesinger's checkup, she didn't even charge the full amount. And her efficient treatment during his one-day stay in the U.S. has turned out to be lifesaving. How would he ever thank her?

On his flight back that evening, Karl remembers that he never gave Ellie that wooden jewelry box he had specifically carved for her. He had never really gotten a chance to unpack his bags. He had spent months making that box just perfect. He would have to mail it to her, though he had really wanted to see her face when she opened such a personal gift. He is disappointed, but knows he needs to get his mind of this.

Then he thinks about his vivid dream about his WWII experiences. He muses about how he has now been rescued and saved a second time by the Americans. He reminisces, as he often does, about his release off that train in Nürnberg that day, October 11, 1945—he will always remember the date of his own liberation. He and most of the boys kissed the ground exuberantly once they had jumped off the train. They hugged each other, said their good-byes and promises to stay in touch, and then all went their own way, each heading in a different direction and all very eager to get home.

Karl had stood on the side of the road with his thumb out to hitchhike home. Very few cars had passed by, as very few roads were completely passable; but finally a guy on a motorbike stopped, and Karl had caught a ride on his back seat, holding on as tightly as he could. He recalls enjoying the wind blowing across his bald head, and he couldn't remember ever feeling more free. But he was anxious to discover what would await him when he got home.

The driver had dropped him approximately two kilometers away from his home, and Karl sprinted the rest.

He had imagined his homecoming with much more fanfare, people out in the street welcoming him, maybe waving at him, cheering him on. But the roads were empty, and there was nobody on the way he could say "hi" to. Nobody was there to welcome him.

In the distance, he saw Opa's house, his childhood home. It was still in one piece. The surrounding houses also stood untouched by bombs. Karl felt instant relief. And smoke rising from their chimney. Someone was home!

He raced down the gravel road as fast as he could toward his home. When he finally reached it, Karl ripped open the downstairs carpentry door and stormed in. *They are still not locking the doors?* Karl fleetingly thought.

Opa was sitting in his usual chair, sanding as if time had stood still for him, though he appeared more gaunt than a year ago.

When he looked up, however, his eyes widened.

"Karl!"

Opa leapt up, the chair in his lap clattering to the floor. As loud as his old, shaky voice allowed him, he screamed in excitement. Karl ran over and embraced him.

"How are you?"

"Good, good and you? You look great!" Opa touched Karl's face as if to inspect him, to make sure he was still in one piece.

"Where is Mutter?" Karl was too excited to wait for an answer—he was already heading towards the steps as he asked the question. He needed to see all his family members, and he already suspected the answer anyway:

"Upstairs!"

Karl found Mutter in the kitchen. She also looked much thinner than she had twelve months ago. She seemed so frail, Karl was afraid he'd crush her as he wrapped his arms around her. He had never hugged her so tight and long, though. Her face was caved in more than when he had last seen her, but it instantly flooded with tears of joy.

"Where are Hermann? Hans?" Flooded with relief that Mutter and Opa were still alive, Karl needed to see his brothers.

"Hermann is his room!" Mutter answered, smiling through her tears.

Karl's eyes widened. "So, he really was brought back the same night they took us?" He had wanted to believe it.

"Yes!"

Ferdinand had told the truth! Karl felt another wave of relief, mixed with the lingering surprise that Ferdinand had brought Hermann right back home, despite Albert's orders. Throughout the war, there were numerous soldiers who remained humane and decent, after all. Karl ran upstairs to find Hermann in his room, sitting in his wheelchair by the window, reading. Hermann's red hair was cut short. The day after his brothers had been taken from their home by the SS, he had asked Mutter to cut it for him, in solidarity with his brothers. He had kept it short ever since. He looked up when he heard Karl enter; his eyes widened, and his mouth was open, smiling the widest grin. Karl smothered his brother with a bear hug, taking care not to pull him out of his wheelchair.

"How have you been? I missed you so much!"

"Great!" Hermann was beyond excited to see his little brother finally back from war. They had worried so much about his whereabouts. Daily he, Mutter, and Opa had prayed for his safe return.

"Have we heard from Hans?" Karl asked. He needed all of his family to be reunited.

But Hermann's big smile faded, and he looked sadly at Mutter, who in the excitement of the reunion had rushed behind Karl up to Hermann's room. Karl followed Hermann's gaze and looked, stricken, at Mutter. His heart sank when he saw her face.

"We've received a letter from the *Abwehr*. Hans was shot and killed in Moscow."

"Moscow? How?"

"We don't know the details."

"Do we know when?"

"No."

Karl doubled over as if someone had punched him really hard and let out the loudest groan: "*Noooooooooo!*"

Mutter rushed over and held him. She mourned silently with him as he cried into her arms.

Then, finally, he looked up at her again. "Did we, or will we, get his body back?"

"No," Mutter shook her head sadly. "He was buried in Moscow along with other German soldiers."

Karl now had confirmation—he had lost his brother Hans in the war. In a way he had always felt it. His gut had told him that he would never see Hans again after the Russians separated them in that field in Linz.

The exact circumstances of how he was killed—or whether he really was killed, or was kept in a camp until he died—were never uncovered. They never found his grave in Moscow, though there were many mass graves. They also never found out the whereabouts of Uncle Joseph, either. He had most likely perished in the war, like so many. By the end of 1954, nine years after the war's end, the German military search service had identified 1,240,629 missing.[2]

Mutter told Karl what had happened that night after Hans and Karl had been taken by the SS:

With only a few more days left to finish the Major's desk, Opa and Mutter had readied the it for pick-up. Everybody, even Hermann, worked many hours to finish it. The Major had showered them with compliments when he saw it; he couldn't have been happier with the outcome. He had paid them with plenty of food ration cards, which then were worth more to them than any *Reichsmark*, though supplies were even harder to come by as it got closer to Germany's defeat and capitulation. The person, who the desk and chair were for, remained a mystery, and they never heard from the Major again— which was just as well for them.

Mutter and Opa also told Karl about the numerous air raid alarms during the last five months of the war. During the first four months of 1945, right before war's end, more bombs were dropped onto Nürnberg than the previous three years combined. More Nürnberg inhabitants died than in the previous war years.

Everyone in the neighborhood used Opa's underground basement as an air raid shelter. One time, fifty people had squeezed into that small space, sitting on top of each other to make room for them all. Fortunately, the house was never hit, though one bomb had detonated in the nearby woods where the kids had always played growing up. It had left a huge crater in their neighboring forest. Nürnberg old town had been hit hard as well, and the old city and the South train station lay in ruins. Not only were 5,000 people killed in the city alone, but over 100,000 were left homeless. Karl remembered the vast destruction he had seen on his train ride in. Mutter talked about the former sand-mill factory only ten kilometers away, which had been turned into a weapons factory the last ten months of the war, and was also eventually bombed. The owner and many factory workers were killed in the air raid. Mutter feared the factory owner and workers would not have been able to live with themselves after the war, since the factory's output directly contributed to prolonging the war and the killing of many. The factory owner and Mutter had been classmates during elementary school.

Karl listened intently as Opa and Mutter went on to tell the story of the American paratrooper who landed in front of Opa's house six months back, completely off course. He had landed hard on their gravel road leading up to their house and was badly injured. Mutter and Opa took care of him for weeks. There were times they weren't sure he would make it; but with the help of Dr. Magdalena, Sr., they nurtured the airman back to health until eventually he was strong enough to join one of his American troops again.

Before the GI left, though, he insisted on shooting a deer for Mutter, Opa, and Hermann in the nearby woods. It was his way of saying thanks to them for saving his life. The venison meat was the first taste of meat they had had in several months, and it lasted them weeks. While they could pick blueberries and mushrooms, and had some potatoes left in storage, neither Opa, Mutter nor Hermann would have been able to hunt for a deer or any other wild game. Even though they still had the food ration cards, the butcher was often out of meat, rendering the food cards mostly useless.

Mutter would always talk about that reciprocating experience as another example of how so many of the soldiers remained humane, even during the war.

****

The pilot of the flight back to Frankfurt, Germany has radioed ahead regarding the heart patient on board in first class. As Karl's flight lands in Frankfurt, an ambulance awaits to take him to the nearby hospital. He is treated like a VIP.

In the ambulance, he hands the written instructions from Dr. Schlesinger to the German medical technicians, to be handed to his doctors. Karl feels confident they will not ignore his health issues any longer.

He is right.

Thanks to that careful and considerate treatment and write-up from Dr. Schlesinger, and the subsequent efficient treatment by the German doctors, Karl will go on to live another decade and a half. He will always claim that the Americans had saved his life a second time.

Back in America, Dr. Schlesinger visits her father the same evening she releases Karl from the hospital. She likes to stop by to have dinner with her father once or twice a week. He is seventy-six now, and he has been a widower for nearly ten years.

"How are the therapy sessions going?" Dr. Schlesinger asks him as he sets the dinner table. Not until recently has he told her more about the details of his tragic experiences as a young man in the German concentration camp Mauthausen. She had known since she was a child that her grandparents had been killed there, and his prisoner number tattoo is still very visible on his forearm. He generally refused to talk about his captivity when she was growing up; but recently he has opened up to her. In doing so, he confirmed what she had always suspected about how badly her father had been tortured there. That he had been beaten and nearly starved to death, while forced to break rock on the Mauthausen quarry for over a year. That his survival was a miracle.

He still doesn't really want to talk to his daughter about it in too much detail, though, and at this point the topic as become taboo. Dr. Schlesinger had recommended that he see a therapist and talk it through there, and he has reluctantly agreed.

"Oh, fine!" he responds to her inquiry, and then, as usual, he doesn't say any more about it. Instead, he changes the subject to the new BBQ chicken recipe he has made today on his Foreman grill. He can't wait for her to try it.

They sit at the table in the dining room of his modest Georgetown townhouse, the remaining sunlight of the sunset streaming onto the dinner table through his large upstairs windows as they enjoy the healthy chicken dinner.

"Mmmhm, this is really good!" she confirms. He smiles, proud that this recipe is yet another success. He loves to cook and to please his hardworking daughter. He wants nothing more than to see her happy. As they eat, she tells him about her day at the office, as she does so often. A retired doctor himself, he knows that she values his input. She tells him about diagnosing this German man with a heart condition. He was in Virginia visiting his daughter, she says. She complains about Germany's socialized medicine and how they were seemingly ignoring Karl's health needs, already having put him on the back burner in Germany at seventy-five. She says his name was "Karl Elheusch".

Dr. Schlesinger's dad looks stunned at the mention of the patient's name. "I used to know a guy named Karl Elheusch," he says. "He lived on my street growing up in Germany,"

His eyes light up. "And he saved me at Mauthausen."

Daniel Morgenthau looks back at his daughter, who is staring at him in wonder. "I wonder if it is the same person. He is a really good guy! Where is he now?"

The End

Epilogue[vi]:

During World War II, over 60 million people were killed—about 3% of the 1940 world population (est. 2.3 billion).[vii]

WWII casualties on the German side were high. The wartime military casualty figures compiled by German High Command, up until January 31, 1945, are often cited by military historians when covering individual campaigns in the war. Post-war German estimates of military deaths range from approximately 4.3 to 5.3 million[viii] armed forces personnel. Civilian deaths during the war include air raid deaths, estimates of German civilians killed only by Allied bombing ranging from around 350,000[ix] to 635,000.[5][6][7] Civilian deaths due to the flight and expulsion of Germans and the forced labor of Germans in the Soviet Union, are disputed and range from 500,000[x] to over 2.0 million[11][12][13][xi] In 2005, the German government Search Service put the total combined German military and civilian war casualties at 7,375,800, including persons of German ancestry who lived outside of the borders of Germany and Austria.[14] This statistic does not include the 200,000 Germans with mental and/or physical disabilities who were murdered in the Nazi euthanasia program.[15]

At the time of WWII, the United States had a large population of ethnic Germans. Among residents of the USA in 1940, more than 1.2 million persons had been born in Germany, 5 million had two native-German parents, and 6 million had one native-German parent. Many more had distant German ancestry. [xii]

References:

i http://www.writing.upenn.edu/library/Parry-Milman_Historical-Medhod_1934.pdf

ii http://www.jmu.edu/stories/cohencenter/2014/09-2014/09-17-mcgann.shtml

iii https://savemetwice.com/2016/11/19/fake-news-propaganda-you-have-been-duped/

iv Richard Grunberger *A Social History of the Third Reich* (1971; London, 1987); 347

v https://en.wikipedia.org/wiki/Mauthausen-Gusen_concentration_camp and "Mauthausen und Befreiung" Gerald Lamprecht

vi https://en.wikipedia.org/wiki/German_casualties_in_World_War_II#cite_note-7

vii https://www.census.gov/population/international/data/worldpop/table_history.php

viii Rüdiger Overmans, Deutsche militärische Verluste im Zweiten Weltkrieg. Oldenbourg 2000. ISBN 3-486-56531-1 page 228

ix Rüdiger Overmans, Deutsche militärische Verluste im Zweiten Weltkrieg. Oldenbourg 2000. ISBN 3-486-56531-1 pp.147-48

x Erich Hampe "Der Zivile Luftschutz im Zweiten Weltkrieg" pp.138-142 The figure of 500,000 includes 436,000 civilians, 39,000 foreign workers and prisoners of war and 25,000 police and military personnel.

xi Die deutschen *Vertreibungsverluste. Bevölkerungsbilanzen für die deutschen Vertreibungsgebiete 1939/50.* Herausgeber: Statistisches Bundesamt - Wiesbaden. Stuttgart: Verlag W. Kohlhammer, 1958

xii https://en.wikipedia.org/wiki/Internment_of_German_Americans http://www.70-jahre-kriegsende.de/

Afterword:

After the war, Karl finished his carpentry apprenticeship and received the title of *"Schreiner Meister"*. He proudly displayed the certificate in his carpentry shop for years.

He went on to produce many quality pieces of furniture, and helped many people in his hometown build their houses (roofs, doors, etc.).

He married and remained married until his wife passed away, decades before his own passing.

Karl told his offspring the stories presented in this book, describing his experiences during World War II, as a sixteen-year-old in the war against his will.

Later in his life, I, his daughter, asked him to write his WWII stories down. I asked him many questions and he either wrote the answers down or I wrote the stories down as told by him. There are many pages of his hand-written notes to back up these stories.

This book is considered fiction based on a true story. The majority of the writing in this book is based on those stories, but I also added some twists and turns of my own.

E. A. Dustin

Made in the USA
Middletown, DE
21 June 2020